STO

FRIENDS
OF ACPL

D1502902

Théodore de Banville

Twayne's World Authors Series

TWAS 700

Théodore de Banville

By Alvin Harms

The University of Calgary

Twayne Publishers • Boston

Théodore de Banville

Alvin Harms

Published by Twayne Publishers
A Division of G. K. Hall & Company
70 Lincoln Street
Boston, Massachusetts 02111

Printed on permanent/durable acid-free paper and bound in the United States of America.

Library of Congress Cataloging in Publication Data

Harms, Alvin.
Théodore de Banville.

(Twayne's world authors series; TWAS 700)
Bibliography: p. 174
Includes index.
1. Banville, Théodore Faullain de, 1823–1891—Criticism and interpretation.
I. Title. II. Series.
PQ2188.H37 1983 841'.8 83-304
ISBN 0-8057-6547-6

Contents

About the Author

Alvin Harms received his B.A. Honors from the University of Saskatchewan and his Ph.D. from the University of Colorado. He was the first head of the Department of Romance Studies at the University of Calgary, where he is now Professor of French. Professor Harms's special interests lie in Romanticism, lyric poetry generally, poetic theory, and ethnic literature in Canada. His publications include articles on Lamartine and Leconte de Lisle and a book on Heredia appearing in 1975 in Twayne's World Authors Series. He has also contributed to the journal _Canadian Ethnic Studies_.

Preface

One of the dangers in preparing a book on a writer who is not well known is the temptation to become a crusader on his behalf, a temptation I have tried to resist. Yet I feel that assessments of Théodore de Banville are too often distorted because they are based on only a small part of his work. Perhaps this is because much of Banville is relatively unknown. I offer this book in the hope that it will contribute some of that knowledge, at least on a basic level, so that any judgment of Banville can derive from the whole of his work. To this end I have attempted to give an indication of the considerable scope of his output--lyric poetry above all, theater, fiction, and poetic theory--as suggested by the various chapter headings. In order to make his numerous collections of poetry better known I have tried to supply at least an adequate notion of their contents and organization.

Apart from the scope of his work, I have attempted to show that verbal virtuosity is only one aspect, and perhaps not the most important one, of his writing. His work is not just empty form. If, as Baudelaire and Mallarmé observe (see Conclusion), Banville is not really a man of his time, he is a man of all times as an incarnation of the lyric poet in the fullest sense of the word. His vision of beauty of form and life is the unifying thread in his work, extending even to his fiction, which is sometimes not read, I suspect, because its existence is unknown.

On the level of literary history, Banville's place needs reexamination. To me it is clear that he is not comfortably placed among the Parnassians, and to the extent that classifications might be desirable, he is, especially on the basis of his poetic theory, a kindred spirit of the Symbolists.

The translations into English are my own, tend to be literal, and do not pretend to reflect the poetic qualities of Banville's verse. For more extended passages of verse I have generally quoted the French original along with my translation. On occasion I have left untranslated passages illustrating play on words, where the whole point would be lost in translation.

Alvin Harms

The University of Calgary

Chronology

1823 Théodore de Banville born March 14 at Moulins-sur-Allier.

1830 Begins studies in October at the Pension Sabatier in Paris.

1834 Banville's parents move to Paris.

1839 Obtains his baccalaureate. Registers for law studies.

1842 Abandons law. *Les Cariatides*.

1845 Joins *La Silhouette*.

1846 His father dies. *Les Stalactites*.

1848 Writes for *Le Pamphlet* followed by *Le Corsaire* and *Le Pouvoir*.

1852 Almost dies from illness. Joins *Le Paris*, where he meets the Goncourts. *Le Feuilleton d'Aristophane*.

1856 *Odelettes*. *Le Beau Léandre*.

1857 Is under the care of Doctor Louis Fleury at Bellevue. Receives government subsidies. *Le Sang de la Coupe*. *Odes Funambulesques*. *Le Cousin du Roi*.

1859 Goes to Nice with actress Marie Daubrun. Writes for *Le Moniteur*. Georges Rochegrosse is born.

1860 Awarded the Légion d'honneur for "La Mer de Nice" and "Nice française," celebrating the annexation of Nice.

1861 *Améthystes*. Collaborates on the *Revue Fantaisiste* of Mendès.

1863 Meets Madame Elisabeth Rochegrosse. *Diane au bois*.

1864 *Les Fourberies de Nérine*.

1865 *La Pomme*.

1866 *Gringoire*. Marries Madame Rochegrosse.

1867 His sister Zélie dies. *Les Exilés*.

1869 *Occidentales*. Becomes theater columnist for *Le National*.

1870 *Florise*.

1872 *Petit Traité de poésie française*.

1874 *Déïdamia*.

1877 *La Perle*.

1878 His mother dies.

1880 Begins writing for *Le Gil Blas*.

1881 *Contes pour les femmes*.

1882 *Contes féeriques*.

1884 *Nous Tous*. *Contes héroïques*. *Riquet à la Houppe*.

1885 *Contes bourgeois*. *Socrate et sa femme*.

1886 *Dames et Demoiselles*.

1887 *Le Forgeron*. *Le Baiser*. *Madame Robert*.

1888 *Les Belles Poupées*. Joins *L'Echo de Paris*.

1890 *Sonnailles et Clochettes*. *Esope*.

1891 *Marcelle Rabe*. Dies on the night of March 12 of pulmonary disease.

1892 *Dans la Fournaise* (posthumously).

Chapter One

Origins and Early Years

Origins

"He was charming! . . . we shall not see him any more, pale, beardless, eyes alert and dark, walking with tiny steps in the sun, rolling his cigarette and greeting people with short little movements . . . ; we shall not see him any more gliding noiselessly, discreet and calm, and yet letting us sense in his whole pattern something rare and exquisite, something fanciful also . . ." (1). This evocative and sensitive portrait came from the pen of Anatole France after the death of Théodore de Banville, whom he calls "the most singing (le plus chantant) of the poets of his time."

Étienne-Claude-Jean-Baptiste-Théodore Faullain de Banville was born at Moulins-sur-Allier on March 14, 1823. His mother's family had lived in the Moulins area since the seventeenth century, perhaps even since the sixteenth. She descended from a long line of legal and finance people. Banville seems to have felt a close temperamental kinship with his maternal great-grandfather, Etienne Dénozier, whose buffoonery and generosity were legendary. Thinking perhaps of his own inclination to spend money imprudently, he recalls his great-grandfather's financial plight in this way: "It was thus that my great-grandfather spent everything, and that is why his great-grandson was reduced to becoming a lyric poet, in order to have a good ray of sunlight for lunch and the wandering breeze and the moonlight for his supper" (2). He imagines a follower of Darwin arguing that he owes to his great-grandfather his "love of lyrical and harmonious buffoonery together with the tender and tumultuous fantasy of his rhymes," to which Banville replies that this is only partly true, for all his relatives had in common the practice of astonishing others by their refusal to adopt commonplace ideas and actions.

The Banville family, known as early as the fifteenth century, established itself in the Cotentin area of Normandy in the sixteenth century. For the most part the Banvilles were men of action, either in military careers or in technical pursuits, and there appears to be no record of any special interest or achievement in the arts within the family before Théodore. It was not until 1780 that the Banvilles took root in Moulins in the person of Jean-Louis Faullain de Banville, a civil engineer, Théodore's grandfather.

Théodore's father, Claude-Théodore de Banville, after two decades in the marine service, retired in Moulins, where he married and worked in the land registry. He was a man of integrity and great dignity, who refused to compromise in matters of justice and beauty. In dedicating his second collection of poems to his father, Banville acknowledges a great indebtedness to him: "I owe everything to the boundless affection with which you protected, defended and supported my childhood, and shaped and enlightened my young soul" (3). He wanted to be worthy of the father who, as he puts it in "A mon père" in that collection, had always held out before him a threefold torch: the ardor for what is good, the hope for what is true, and the love for what is beautiful.

If Banville admired his father, he adored his mother. She must have been a woman of unusual quality, and if she represented his ideal of womanhood, he must have found few women to equal such an image. To her Banville dedicated not only his first collection of verse, <u>Les Cariatides</u>, but also a later one entitled <u>Roses de Noël</u>. In addition, references to her abound in poems scattered in other collections. She was fond of the arts, especially poetry and painting, and even wrote some verse herself. Judging from Banville's references to her, she possessed every important virtue. Even if we allow for some idealization it is clear that she was tenderly devoted to her family and left her children many cherished memories. But perhaps her most striking quality was her positive attitude toward life, her cheerfulness, and her enthusiasm. These her son also possessed.

A Happy Childhood

Théodore de Banville could hardly have had a better beginning. The world into which he was born was warm and protective. The family lived at 35 rue de Bourgogne in an old aristocratic dwelling behind which was a large garden, which he was to recall nostalgically later in less idyllic circumstances in Paris: "I lived in rooms which, with a bed, a little table, and three volumes of poetry, were infinitely too abundantly furnished; but there I saw time and time again in my dreams the large garden of Bourgogne Street, where tortoises crept slowly in the sand, and my little sister Zélie, rosy as she fled into the light, and my adorable grandmother, who had given me the birds, the fish, the frogs, the dragonflies, and that whole big ecstatic paradise of greenery and flowers" (4).

His maternal grandparents lived only a few steps away. He and his little sister (who was two years older than he), the only children in the family, spent as much time there as in their parents' house. According to Banville, he never did decide in which of the two houses he belonged. After the death of his grandfather, when Théodore was only two, his grandmother lived almost solely for her grandchildren and, as Banville puts it, spoiled them beyond words, believing as had her husband and Banville's parents, that it was necessary to give as much happiness to little children as possible because they might not have any later in life. And besides, according to his grandfather's theories, those who as children had been treated with much tenderness and love would be able later in life to withstand tribulation, while those who had been harshly treated in childhood would never recover and even in favorable circumstances in later life would suffer from these bad memories. Banville remembers dining regularly twice a day first at his grandmother's house and then at his own. In this way he fortified himself for later life when, as he recalls, he often had to dine "from memory."

Moulins itself was for him a gay, dreamy, and picturesque town, "to be adored passionately." It was a place in which time did not matter. Peasant women in their quaint, old-fashioned clothes had something vaguely medieval about them. In marked contrast to "that fever of unrest which consumes everyone in Paris" not much happened here. Modern technology had not yet destroyed the past in Moulins. In this happy place the scholar, the archaeologist, and the poet could find the deep peace needed for their work (5).

Not far from Moulins there was an idyllic country property composed of a vineyard and orchard, cultivated land, meadows, a stream flowing past the owner's dwelling, and a fountain whose water was reputed among the peasants of the region to have healing powers. This property, known as La Font-Georges, had been bought by Banville's maternal grandfather to please his daughter, so that she could eat the fruit of its century-old sorb apple tree. La Font-Georges, enchantment of his childhood, inspired Banville to celebrate it in several poems, one of which Sainte-Beuve was later to praise for its moving qualities and to compare with Ronsard's "De l'élection de mon sépulcre" and with that poet's verses written to the Fontaine Bellerie (6). Moulins and La Font-Georges, these formed the twofold paradise of Théodore's earliest memories. In "Bien souvent je revois . . . ," a poem dated 1841, from _Les Cariatides_, he evokes in quasi-Lamartinean accents Moulins with its nostalgic charms:

> Ce vieux pont de granit bâti par mon aïeul,
> Nos fontaines, les champs, les bois, les chères
> tombes,
> Le ciel de mon enfance où volent les colombes,
> Les larges tapis d'herbe où l'on m'a promené
> Tout petit, la maison riante où je suis né. . .
> (v. 5, p. 198)

> (That old bridge built by my grandfather, our fountains, the fields, the woods, the dear tombs, the sky of my childhood where doves flew, the broad carpets of grass where I was taken on walks when I was very small, the cheery house where I was born. . .)

Then he sees the streets and the road leading to La Font-Georges linked with a flood of memories crowding in on him: the sorb apple tree, the poplars, the spring gushing from the moss, his sister Zélie, the old vineyard workers, the bees golden in the sunlight, the orchard full of birds, songs, murmurings, the peach trees with their ripe fruit, and even the joyful barking of his dog Calisto.

In this setting, experiencing the warmth and gentle love of grandparents and parents, themselves living in unusual harmony, and in the company of his sister, "spreading gayety and light around her," Théodore was as happy as in a fairy-tale world. Even when we allow for his penchant for hyperbole and when we consider that his memory may well have reconstituted a poetic past rather than a historical one, there is little doubt that his childhood was an unusually happy one.

The Pension Sabatier

Two events in 1830 brought his carefree existence to an abrupt end. One of them was the death of his grandmother; the other was the decision to send the seven-year-old Théodore to the Pension Sabatier, a boarding school situated at 9 rue Richer in Paris. In referring to this part of his life he speaks of his "captivity" and compares himself to "a little wild animal." What he found there was repressed enthusiasm, hurt feelings, the triumph of mediocrity and the banal, dirty classrooms, and among the teachers ignorance, cruelty, and martyrdom. Even the grounds ("notre jardin," they were called) seemed ragged, barren, and gloomy. The trees were planted all in a row like bowling pins and there were no fruit trees, no bodies of water, no dragonflies, no birds except Parisian sparrows, ironic and bantering like the other schoolboys. Banville's account leads us to believe that he did not fit in well with the other boys, most of whom were from rich families. He relates, for example, how he suffered during school recesses, when instead of participating in the play of the others he would pace back and forth like a caged animal. Holidays and Sundays seemed interminable (7).

To make matters even worse, the food was grossly inferior in quality to the sumptuous feasts prepared by his grandmother or to the skillful and refined cooking of Nanette Coudour, the maid of the Banvilles. Instead of these delicacies, he found at the boarding school soups that were clear as a silvery brook, sorry fish, anemic meat, underbaked bread sometimes ten days old, hard in the middle but with its crust softened from damp storage. Even amusements and entertainment were regimented. Every year the school observed the birthday of the director with a gift for which money was collected from the students, who of course had no voice in the choice of the gift. The whole school would gather in the garden under strict supervision. The director for his part, in return for this celebration, treated the students to an evening at the Théâtre Comte, to which they marched in a body and in line. Once there, Banville would suffer from the childish comedies with their less than subtle puns. Even worse were the magic tricks of Monsieur Comte. Banville had an unusually good memory and he found it painful from one performance to the next to hear over and over again the same puns, the same commentaries, and the same jokes, the punch lines of which he remembered from the first time.

Still the years at the Pension Sabatier had their brighter moments too. If Théodore felt that he did not fit in with the rest of the boys, he learned from them to take things as they came and to regard life from the perspective of comedy. In the same sentence in which he mentions the horror of these years he also states that the pension was run by a very likable family, which fussed over him like a son. And although he was often lonely he was frequently invited out. Friends and relatives took him to the theater, and he had the good fortune to see the amazing equilibrist Madame Saqui perform. A teacher of Greek, an older man, with a taste for Aristophanes and theater generally, befriended Banville and often took him to see plays and other dramatic performances including those of the clown Odry.

The director of the school treated the boys not only to an evening at the Théâtre Comte but also to an afternoon performance by the Grimacier, a mime, who with nothing but a crownless hat was able to present an endless variety of comedy. By means of movements of his nose, eyes, and mouth he appeared to be able to mold his face into new expressions at will, thereby creating a "perpetual and changing caricature of himself and of foolish humanity." At the same time his fingers would knead his hat into countless unexpected shapes to accompany his facial expressions. Through this skillful combination he was able to portray the whole human race in an endless variety of its individual incarnations. He was "all the types that exist between God and animals, represented and made fun of with a verve which resembled genius and with the most astonishing and merciless exactness" (8).

This poor wretch, this Pierrot-like figure, immediately won Banville's sympathy and admiration. There was something touching about him. It is easy to imagine the young Banville watching every move of the Grimacier with wide-eyed wonder, perhaps without understanding the deeper cause of his fascination, but on looking back, Banville was to see in this man and his art the very embodiment of the poet: "And what else is the life of the artist and the poet, especially the poet, who offers himself, gives himself, shapes his soul like clay, and has to play his comedy without stage sets, without costumes, without any material aid, and still must give the illusion of everything that lives and breathes, without letting anything show except his mind?" (9).

The Grimacier's impression on Banville was lasting. All his life Banville was to be fascinated by acrobats, clowns, mimes, and tightrope walkers; and he himself became in a sense a verbal acrobat in some of his work. From an early age, love of the theater seems to have been in his blood. The pupils of the Pension Sabatier were sometimes taken to a children's theater first called the Théâtre Joly and later known as the Gymnase enfantin. Here he admired the enthusiasm of the young audience and its feeling of participation in the action of the plays, which were heavily charged with elements of fancy and of mime. But what especially thrilled Banville was the Théâtre des Funambules on the boulevard du Temple. "If I except the incomparable joys of poetry and of love," he says, "the hours that I spent in this smoky little hall were certainly the best of my existence" (10). Here he saw the great Jean-Gaspard Deburau, peerless clown and mime, whose interpretation of Pierrot was delightfully lyrical and comical. At the end of a charming _dizain_ entitled "Pierrot" in _Les Cariatides_ Banville captures something of this spirit as he pictures the actor walking along the boulevard du Temple after a performance: "La blanche Lune aux cornes de taureau / Jette un regard de son oeil en coulisse / A son ami Jean Gaspard Deburau" (v. 5, p. 248) (The white moon with horns of a bull casts a glance into the wings at its friend Jean Gaspard Deburau).

After four years in Paris Banville was reunited with his family when the latter took residence on the rue des Fosses-Saint-Jacques. Moulins had become noticeably cool toward Théodore's father, whose stand on certain political issues had made him unpopular. Théodore meanwhile continued his studies at the Pension Sabatier, obtaining his baccalaureate late in 1839. His next step was to begin law studies. He managed to take his first examinations but abandoned law permanently in 1842, giving up "codes" for "odes," as he put it.

It is not clear why he should have begun law studies in the first place. Certainly his parents did not press him to do so. On the contrary, his mother encouraged him to be a poet. Banville himself appears to have known from early childhood that he would be one and in fact felt compelled by destiny to follow that path. Not by nature a boastful person he was nonetheless proud to be a poet. In recalling his childhood he relates the idyllic setting of La Font-Georges to his poetic calling: ". . . in the moonlight the fairies would come to dance and sing beside the murmuring spring, and as I myself often slept there, lying in the grass, it was doubtless at such times that they kissed my childish lips and communicated to me the divine and incurable fever of poetry" (11). He felt himself not only preordained to be a poet but also incapable of resisting this election. And it was a point of honor for him to have remained faithful to his calling. More than twenty years after the publication of his first collection of poetry he reminds the Muse of his continuing devotion:

> Je n'ai pas renié la Lyre. Je puis boire
> Encore dans la fontaine à la profondeur
> noire
> Où le Rhythme [sic] soupire avec les flots
> divins.
> O Déesse, j'étais un enfant quand tu vins
> Pour la première fois baiser ma chevelure.
> J'étais comme un avril en fleur. Nulle
> souillure
> Ne tachait la fierté de mon coeur ingénu.
> Plus de vingt ans se sont passés: mon front
> est nu. (12)

(I have not renounced the Lyre. I can still drink at the fountain with its dark depths where Rhythm sighs with the divine springs. O Goddess, I was a child when you came for the first time to kiss my hair. I was like an April in bloom. No blemish stained the pride of my innocent heart. More than twenty years have passed; my brow is bald.)

He ends the poem by recalling that twenty others who also had sworn to be true to the Muse forever have all deserted her and he is the only one who has remained faithful.

Although Banville was not a brilliant student, his school days had not been a waste of time for him. On the contrary, it is obvious in retrospect that they had been an invaluable preparation for his poetic career. His contact with theater nourished his taste for it and gave him the opportunity to become familiar with it, so that even at an early age he was reflecting on its nature and was beginning to formulate rather mature opinions and theories about it. Along with theater and possibly also through it he was acquiring knowledge about life in Paris and life in general. Perhaps more important still was the fact that school gave him the opportunity to read. The writers he had read before leaving school ranged from Homer to Musset, and included Vergil, Ovid, Shakespeare, Clément Marot, Pierre de Ronsard, E. T. A. Hoffmann, Alfred de Vigny, Hugo, and perhaps others. His Greek teacher had introduced him to Aristophanes, a playwright for whom he had an affinity. The Shakespeare that appealed to him especially was the Shakespeare of the lighter, airy, and fanciful plays such as A Midsummer Night's Dream and As You Like It. Curiously one of the first writers Banville read was Boileau. If this choice seems surprising, there being little kinship of spirit between him and Boileau, the explanation is quite simple: Boileau was the only poet available to him at the beginning. "I knew entirely by heart the works of Boileau," he tells us, "the only poet, alas, at my disposal" (13). The significance of the word "alas," a reflection of his reaction to Boileau, was later to be developed in more detail in his treatise on poetry. On the other hand, the poet who made the greatest impact on him and at whose shrine he never ceased to worship was Victor Hugo.

Chapter Two
Les Cariatides

An Overview

Not only had Banville read extensively by the time he left the Pension Sabatier, but he had also begun to write verse. His first collection, *Les Cariatides*, was published in 1842, the year he abandoned law studies. The volume appeared during a noticeable lull in the publication of first-rate poetry in France. If we except such works as Hugo's *Les Rayons et les Ombres* and Théophile Gautier's *España*, no major collections of verse appeared in France in the 1840s. The first wave of Romantic poetry had passed. Lamartine and Alfred de Musset had very nearly come to the end of their productivity in poetry. Vigny, although he produced a number of major poems during these years, did not publish his *Destinées* until two decades later. Hugo was straddling the watershed of thirteen years between *Les Rayons et les Ombres* and *Les Châtiments* of 1853. Gautier's *Emaux et Camées* and all of Gérard de Nerval's major poetry were published in the 1850s. Neither Baudelaire nor Leconte de Lisle, both only slightly older than Banville, published a major volume of poetry until the 1850s. In a sense the 1840s could be regarded as a period of transition. Changes were in the air. The age of Lamartine was ending and the seeds of Parnassianism and Symbolism were germinating.

Although Banville apparently began writing poetry at the age of sixteen, most of the poems in *Les Cariatides*, a collection of some five thousand verses, are dated 1842. At first glance, this volume appears to be a confusing mixture of poems, but it fits almost perfectly into its historic setting, restating and prolonging a number of Romantic creeds, at times observing the idea of art for art's sake, and at others practicing the cult of antiquity. Not only does the collection contain *en germe* his later poetic works but it is a kind of microcosm of the history of French poetry in the nineteenth century. If the collection seems confusing and sometimes contradictory, it must be remembered that it is the product of youth. Enthusiasm and spontaneity are often not tempered by discipline and mature judgment. Banville in a preface of 1877 makes no apologies for it: "Of all the books I have written, this is the only one for which I do not need to ask indulgence, for I had the fortune to finish it between my sixteenth and my eighteenth year, that is to say, that divinely unselfconscious age when we really experience the intoxication of the Muse and when the poet produces odes as a rose bush produces roses" (1).

The analogy with the rose bush seems singularly inapt when applied to Les Cariatides; it would be more accurate to say that some of the poems are produced after the manner of Gautier or André Chénier or Marceline Desbordes-Valmore or Marot or Musset, especially Musset. Epigraphs accompanying many of the poems and chosen from a wide range of sources--Hesiod, Ovid, Vergil, the Apocalypse, Shakespeare, Ronsard, Joachim Du Bellay, Racine, Molière, Goethe, Hugo, and Gautier--perhaps reflect some of the influences to which he had been exposed. It is difficult to discover the originality of Banville in this book. That he could versify with a certain ease is already evident and that he could with equal ease imitate the forms, rhythms, and subject matter of other poets is also clear. Indeed Les Cariatides might strike the reader as a kind of potpourri, so diverse is it in tone, form, and subject matter.

The opening poem, dedicating the volume to his mother, expresses Banville's wish that she might find in the book all the hopes of his youth and a revelation of his thoughts and feelings:

> Le vague et lointain souvenir
> De mon enfance dépensée
> Dans un rêve triste et moqueur,
> Fou, car il contient ma pensée,
> Chaste, car il contient mon coeur.
> (v. 5, p. 2)

(The vague and distant memory of my childhood spent in a sad and mocking dream, foolish, for it contains my thought, chaste, for it contains my heart.)

The adjectives "triste," "moqueur," "fou," and "chaste" are significant for they point to two constantly appearing visages of the poet: on the one hand, Banville the clown, the verbal acrobat, the humorist; and on the other, Banville the earth-bound exile thirsting for a state more elevated and pure than that in which he finds himself.

The dedication is followed by a key poem, "Les Cariatides." The Cariatides in question here are the sculptured columns in the shape of women that support the temple of Apollo underneath whose portals "the heroes and the gods of love will pass." In addition to giving the collection its title, the poem contains indications of some of the important elements of the book: the cult of sculptured form, the love of antiquity and its mythologies, the thirst for the ideal, the joys and suffering of love, the martyrdom of those whom Banville will call exiles, and the role of the poet. Suggestions of the hardness and durability of matter and form are contained not only in the title, which anticipates such comparable titles as *Les Stalactytes*, *Améthystes*, and Gautier's *Emaux et Camées*, but also in phrases such as *filles de Paros* ("daughters of Paros"), *sage ciseleur* ("wise sculptor"), *ces médaillons* ("these medallions"), *mâle ciseau* ("masculine chisel"), and *figures d'ivoire* ("figures of ivory"), expressions bringing to mind Gautier's "L'Art," which was to appear in 1857. But the concept of frozen beauty does not harmonize with Banville's temperament. His Vénus de Milo in the poem of the same title is sensuous enough to make us forget that she is a statue. In spite of the phrase "grand poème de pierre" with which Banville characterizes her, there is life and voluptuousness in her, a feeling which the poet expresses in lines which might have come from the pen of Baudelaire: "Et vous m'étaleriez votre ventre indompté, / Pour y dormir un soir comme un amant sculpté!" (v. 5, p. 225) (And you would spread out your unconquered belly for me to sleep there some evening like a sculptured lover). How immobile Leconte de Lisle's Vénus de Milo seems by comparison!

The procession of heroes and gods of love referred to in "Les Cariatides" includes among others Orpheus, father of poets, and Aphrodite. They represent a heroic age and elevated ideals. These are values for which the poet longs and whose passing he regrets. Now even nature seems strangely empty and dying without its gods:

Nature, où sont tes Dieux? O prophétique
  aïeule,
O chair mystérieuse où tout est contenu,
Qui pendant si longtemps as vécu de toi
  seule
Et qui sembles mourir, parle, qu'est
  devenu
Cet âge de vertu que chaque jour efface,
Où le sourire humain rayonnait sur ta
  face?
Où s'est enfui le choeur des Olympiens?
(v. 5, p. 219)

(Nature, where are your Gods? Oh prophetic ancestor, oh mysterious flesh in which all is contained, you who have for so long lived off yourself and who seem to be dying, speak. What has become of that virtue erased by each day when a human smile brightened your face? Where has the chorus of Olympians fled?)

These lines, somewhat heavily charged with exclamations, form the opening of the poem "Erato." As was the case for the Musset of "Rolla," for Leconte de Lisle, and for many others, life appears empty without the gods, especially those of Greek mythology. But unlike many, perhaps most, of the French poets of this time, Banville did not feel that Christianity was an outworn creed. A practicing Roman Catholic, he was for a time a church warden in the parish of Saint-Germain-des-Prés. He states his faith in God in his typically amusing and witty manner: "I ardently believe in God and doubtless I am within my rights, for, as one of my atheist friends so well explained to me, versifiers, purely instinctive beings, are not expected to have as much reasoning power as adults and lack the necessary comprehension to picture vast spaces inhabited by nothing at all" (2).

Another striking difference is Banville's refusal to despair. If the gods have fled, the poet with the help of the Muse Erato can bring them back. He calls on the Muse, who chose him when he was yet a child "pour les vers et pour le chant lyrique" to come:

Viens! ceux qu'on a crus morts, nous les
  retrouverons!

Les guerriers, les archers, les rois, les
forgerons,
Les reines de l'azur aux fronts baignés
d'aurore!
Viens, nous retrouverons le fils des rois
Titans. . .
(v. 5, pp. 222-23)

(Come! We shall find again those whom we thought dead. The warriors, the archers, the kings, the smiths, the queen of the azure skies with brows bathed in the light of dawn! Come, we shall find again the son of the Titan kings . . .)

Then follows an enumeration of other figures to be brought back.

This nostalgia for the age of the beginning of human life is accentuated for Banville by the imperfections he sees in his own time. His most explicit criticisms are probably found in "Nostalgie," a poem of thirteen quatrains all together forming a single sentence, an early example of Banville's mastery of language. The first eight quatrains consist of a series of subordinate clauses, while the last five are made up of the principal clause Que ne puis-je ("Why can I not"), followed by a series of infinitive phrases. The group of subordinate clauses produces an oppressive heaviness and a cumulative effect suggesting an abundance of woes beyond those that are really named. The ills he mentions can be summarized as the spirit of materialism in the world of affairs and also in the arts, where anything cheap or appealing to popular taste is repugnant to him. How much better it would be, the last part of the poem suggests, to flee from Paris and to go back in time to live in a world inhabited by nymphs and satyrs.

Banville's vision of animated nature together with his Christianity leads to some curious mixtures of pagan and Christian elements. He does not appear to accept François-René de Chateaubriand's view that mythological beings tend to destroy the splendor and solitude of nature. Rather, he is convinced that they add to its charms and constitute its very life. But for him they are not incompatible with Christian elements. In "La Nuit de printemps," sylphs, undines, Ariel, and Zephyrus coexist comfortably with seraphim, cherubim, the Virgin Mary, and the Christian God. An early example of Banville's lighter vein, this poem is written in airy seven-syllable verse. Its epigraph, a well-known passage beginning with "If we shadows have offended. . ." from Shakespeare's A Midsummer Night's Dream, alerts the reader to his fanciful approach, and the general tone recalls that of Musset in such poems as "Ballade à la lune." The sun is compared to Harlequin and its sister the moon is called "Mademoiselle la Lune." Meanwhile, from his lofty throne, God, benign and lordly, tolerantly watches His children, not deigning to interfere in their childlike activities. The sylphs and cherubim have been charged with producing the month of May to please the Virgin, and so they give pistils and perfume to the flowers, leaves to the trees, song to the nightingale, flight and color to the butterfly, and golden rhymes to the poet. Light and fanciful as this vision is, Banville is not making fun of it. It does not surprise him, and seems as natural to him as it did to see fairies in his boyhood La Font-Georges.

Although there breathes in this poem and in others a certain spirit of innocence and perhaps even naiveté, Banville is not unaware of the ugly aspects of life. In "Auguste Supersac," whose rhythmic structure and abundance of subordinate clauses recall "Nostalgie," he addresses himself to the problem of evil:

> Pourquoi partout le mal vient-il donc à son tour?
> Près du berceau la tombe,
> Le bourbier près du flot de cristal, le vautour
> Auprès de la colombe?
> (v. 5, p. 241)

> (Why then does evil come everywhere in its turn? Next to the cradle, the tomb, the mud next to the crystal stream, the vulture near the dove?)

He provides no answer, except that our salvation consists in turning to the good and the beautiful, and these we have in our soul:

> Les chansons des oiseaux chez nous expatriés,
> Les transparents gazes,
> Les tulipes en or, les champs coloriés,
> Les caprices des vases,
> Les lyres, les chansons, les horizons de feu,

Le zéphir qui se pâme!
Pourquoi chercher ailleurs l'azur du pays bleu?
Nous l'avons dans notre âme.
(v. 5, p. 242)

(Songs of the birds exiled among us, transparent veils, golden tulips, fields in color, capricious vases, lyres, songs, fiery horizons, the fainting zephyr! Why seek elsewhere the azure of the blue homeland? We have it in our soul.)

What might appear as a lack of serious concern in Banville about the evils of this world is rather a poetic and childlike innocence, a happy faculty of seeing beauty everywhere amid ugliness and imperfection.

Women and Love

Les Cariatides contains virtually no verse that can be perceived as arising from any personal experience of love on Banville's part, no expression of nostalgia for a youthful sweetheart, no note of regret for a lost love, no cry of pain or joy. There is a notable scarcity of reports about love affairs in his life. Near the end of his studies in Paris he apparently fell in love with one of Zélie's friends whom he saw during his vacations at Moulins. But this brief idyll has left scarcely any trace in Les Cariatides. It is true that in "Songe d'hiver" the narrator recalls a forgotten time when "the soul of a woman linked to [his] soul had broken it," and there is a reference in "Les Baisers de pierre" to a girl named Judith. But it is not clear how much of this is taken from his own life.

The lack of personal inspiration, however, does not prevent love from being a significant theme in Les Cariatides. One of the gods of love in the procession in the title poem is Eros, "le bienfaiteur et le pâle assassin" (the benefactor and the pale murderer). These two attributes point to two ways of envisaging love and women, a conception which, needless to say, is not original with Banville.

On the one hand we find, as in "Amour angélique," a pure, chaste, and childlike being recalling the Virgin Mary:

L'ange aimé qu'ici-bas je révère et je prie
Est une enfant voilée avec ses longs cheveux,

A qui le ciel, pour qu'elle nous sourie,
A donné le regard de la vierge Marie.
(v. 5, p. 193)

(The beloved angel whom I revere and to whom I pray here is a child veiled with her long hair to whom heaven has given the expression of the Virgin Mary so that she may smile at us.)

However, such an innocent soul is really not of this earth, but rather a messenger from heaven, pure as the flowers of the meadow.

"L'Auréole" shows us another aspect of this ideal type of maiden, namely, the power of her quasi-divine purity to disarm even the most resolute seducers. The setting is an elegant ballroom. The atmosphere is laden with sensuous music and perfumes. As the ball nears its end, the would-be Don Juans are eyeing the ladies and already savoring the pleasures of their conquests. The narrator notices a young lady of such striking beauty that he forgets all the others. He searches in himself how best to seduce her, but when he approaches her all his plans are dispelled:

Mais quand je m'approchai je vis sa tête ceinte
D'un tel rayonnement de pudeur grave et sainte,
Il était si divin, le rhythme de ses pas,
Que, don Juan dérouté, je n'osai même pas
Comme le docteur Faust, en me penchant vers elle,
Lui dire à demi-voix: Ma belle demoiselle!
(v. 5, p. 214)

(But when I approached I saw her head wreathed in such a radiance of grave and holy modesty, it was so divine, the rhythm of her steps, that I, a Don Juan put to rout, did not even dare, like Dr. Faust, to lean toward her and say to her softly: My lovely lady!)

The female figures in Les Cariatides are often drawn from literature and mythology. "En habit Zinzolin," for example, consists of eight short poems composed of rondeaux, triolets, and madrigals, old verse forms underlining the historical distance between the reader and the eight nymphs and maidens to whom the poems are addressed. The tone is light and graceful, and the thought centers with a discreet sensuousness on the physical beauty and grace of these figures. At times the poems recall classical pastoral verse and at others they are more reminiscent of the _galant_ poetry of the seventeenth century.

Quite a different conception emerges in "Les Baisers de pierre," a rather lengthy, perhaps too lengthy, poem recalling Byron and the Musset of "Rolla" and "Mardoche." It is written in the form of a _causerie familière_, an easy confidential chatting style with numerous digressions which allow the narrator to comment on the events and to contribute his own ideas. He relates the story of a young man who deteriorates morally after having been betrayed by the first girl he has ever loved. The protagonists of this _conte moral_ are the sixteen-year-old Prosper and his cousin Judith, dainty, beautiful, and seemingly virtuous. Prosper falls in love with her. They have a first rendezvous in a dark lane. At this point the narrator celebrates in a series of exclamations the joys of innocent first love. Another meeting follows. The intoxication of the senses mounts. Suddenly a series of family deaths puts an end to their meetings. "What a large number of deaths at once," exclaims the narrator. "It's like a melodrama." Judith's father marries her off to a pompous young diplomat. Prosper has another rendezvous with her while her husband is away. Unexpectedly he returns and Judith screams in a successful attempt to make him believe she is being attacked. Prosper is thrown out of the house.

After this betrayal he abandons himself to a life of debauchery, "plunging himself alive into a sea of women," as Banville puts it. He reaches the depths of degradation in his relationship with a satanic, vampirelike woman who delights in drinking the blood of her victim. Prosper escapes from her and takes stock of himself. Realizing that his former self is dead, he goes in search of memories of his better past. He can no longer be a poet, for his dissolute life has left his heart empty and false. He cannot even continue to be a Don Juan. On a typically Banvillean note of satire, his final humiliation is that he becomes a vaudevillean.

The Poet

As early as _Les Cariatides_ it becomes clear that

love is not Banville's most important literary theme. The twelve-part poem "Songe d'hiver" relates a dream in which two women, both exceptionally beautiful, come to the narrator. The first one, a blonde, invites him to share with her a life of pleasure. The second one, a pale woman, offers him her eternal and chaste love in a marble bed in which he will sleep forever. At this point a golden-haired maiden with a luminous and perfumed radiance appears carrying a lyre. The narrator's room is transformed into a palace in which he witnesses the feasting and the orgies of the world's Don Juans and Venuses. In this context Banville inserts a short history of the literary Don Juans and also of the Venuses, women of legendary beauty, present at the feast. All fall victim first to the blonde woman and then to the pale one. About to succumb in his turn, the narrator is held back by the golden-haired maiden, who reveals to him the identity of the other two: one is Volupté (sensual pleasure) and the other is Mort (death). When he wakes up from his nightmare all these visions have fled except for Poetry, the golden-haired maiden, and ever since, he says, it is the child with the lyre and her celestial love whom he has followed.

Indeed the one subject that obsesses Banville in almost everything he writes--poetry, theater, prose fiction, or criticism--is poetry and the poet. In the title poem of Les Cariatides the speaker announces that he, solicitous of the glory of the heroes and gods, wishes to repair the laurel wreaths that crown their heads. The first hero in the procession is Orpheus, the father of poetry. The longest poem of the collection, the poem that forms its core, so to speak, "La Voie lactée," is in part an apology of orphic art and among other things a kind of poetic manifesto. A considerable part of the poem appears to owe its inspiration to Ovid. Not only does it bear an epigraph from his Metamorphoses suggesting the title "La Voie lactée," but it contains an adaptation of the episode of the golden age. Banville sees the Voie Lactée ("Milky Way") as the image of poetry, a way of triumph and joy whose serene and celestial splendor, seemingly consisting of a single body of light, is really made up of myriads of stars. Telle est la poésie ("Such is poetry"), he explains. In the distance it appears as a vast and confusing body of light. But it is possible to discern the individual stars that form it.

The first of these is Orpheus, archetype of the poet, singer, and charmer of all nature in a golden and undefiled age. But Orpheus is destined to suffer. He loses his Eurydice, image of happiness and beauty, which in this earthly life is revealed only in a fleeting dream. As a symbolic figure Orpheus shows that it is the poet's fate to suffer. He is keenly aware of the discrepancy between reality and his vision of beauty. But it is also his destiny, divinely decreed, to suffer. This image of the poet as a superior suffering being, endowed with the power and mission to reveal to humanity a more lofty path, is basically a Romantic conception, to which Banville returns frequently in his writing.

The Orpheus episode is followed by a rapid sketch of the history of poetry, including the following names: Homer, Sophocles, Aeschylus, Aristophanes, Sappho, Lucretius, Horace, Virgil, Menander, Plautus, Lucan, Terence, Tasso, Dante, Ariosto, Shakespeare, Ronsard, Milton, Camoëns, Corneille, Racine, La Fontaine, Molière, Goethe, Schiller, Lamartine, Deschamps, Sainte-Beuve, Vigny, Byron, Musset, Barbier, Moreau, Desbordes-Valmore, Delphine Gay, Laprade, Méry, Brizeux, Gautier, Heine, and Hugo. These are the successors of Orpheus, the other stars of the Milky Way. The list is so long that Banville does little more than record the names with brief comments. Occasionally he dwells a little longer on a poet. For instance, he expresses his admiration for the charm of Shakespeare's fairy and dream world. But he gives the largest share of his attention to Victor Hugo, whom curiously he never mentions by name.

Throughout his life Banville continued to regard Hugo as the greatest of modern poets and as a model to be followed by anyone aspiring to be a poet. Obviously in "La Voie lactée" Banville does just that. His ideas about Hugo are taken from Hugo's *Préface de Cromwell* and especially from the preface to his *Les Voix intérieures*. In the latter he writes, "And in the age in which we live is not all of man to be found there? Is he not entirely contained in this threefold aspect of our life: the home, the field, the street? The home, which is our very heart, the field, where nature speaks to us, the street, where. . . political events rage" (3). The verse "Triple aspect du foyer, du champ et de la rue" (threefold aspect of the home, the field, and the street) occurs more than once in "La Voie lactée" and its comments about Hugo consist of an elaboration of this threefold aspect of man.

In spite of his great admiration for Hugo there is one side of Banville's conception of the poet where his views are closer to those of Vigny and many of the writers of the middle years of the nineteenth century. This has to do with the relationship between the poet and society. Hugo and Lamartine do not appear to have suffered from any perception of a gulf between them and society, but Vigny's view of the poet as a solitary pariah is well known. Although Banville regards the poet's mission as a lofty one, he does not look upon him as a prophet in the sense that some of the great Romantics do. Like Vigny, however, he sees the poet as an outcast from a society whose materialistic values prevent him from fulfilling his role. In "La Mort du poète" the dying poet, reliving his dreams and unrealized ideals, recalls

> . . . le moment fatal où tous ceux de la terre,
> De la plaine et des monts,
> Avaient dit: Tu n'es pas, ô reveur solitaire,
> De ceux que nous aimons!
> (v. 5, p. 161)

> (the fatal moment when all those of the earth, of the plain and of the mountains had said: You are not, oh solitary dreamer, one of those whom we love!)

This isolation within a society that cares nothing for the poet's values is of course one important dimension of the suffering to which he is doomed. The image of the pariah is found several times in Les Cariatides. "La Lyre morte," for example, refers to the poet as one of the animals forgotten by Buffon, an animal of whom the public makes a clown fit only to entertain near the end of a feast. In "Les deux frères" we find this statement about poetry: "La vaste Poésie est faite avec deux choses: / Une Ame, champ brûlé que fécondent les pleurs, / Puis une Lyre d'or, écho de ces douleurs / . . ." (v. 5, p. 169) (Vast Poetry is made with two things: A Soul, burned field fertilized by tears, and a Lyre of gold, the echo of these sufferings). The two brothers designated by the title represent the soul and the lyre. By their nature they must suffer and be outcasts, "Deux nobles parias, en un mot deux poètes" (Two noble pariahs, in a word two poets). "Sous bois" underlines the poet's lowly social status in another way. Here we find in a forest setting a curiously mixed procession of actors incarnating such diverse roles as Herod, Adonis, Hippolytus, Cleopatra, and Pierrot. Right at the end of the procession, looking sad and dreamy, come the poet and the donkey. The meeting of poet and donkey, which we find again in Francis Jammes, brings together outcasts from the world of men and animals respectively, and by association with Christ and the donkey in Jerusalem points to the greatness of the poet as well as to his humility.

Banville shares the Romantic view of the poet as a Christlike figure, sacrificing himself in order to give to humanity a priceless gift. This image is suggested in "Le Pressoir," which compares the poet's heart to grapes crushed by a blind machine, leaving only formless pulp:

> Que le coeur du poète et la grappe qu'on
>   souille
> Ne soient plus qu'une triste et honteuse
>   dépouille,
> Qu'importe, si pour tous, au bruit d'un chant
>   divin,
> Ruisselle éblouissant le flot sacré du vin!
> (v. 5, p. 235)

(What does it matter that the heart of the poet and the grapes that are defiled are no longer anything but a sad and shameful pulp, as long as the dazzling stream of wine gushes forth for all to the sound of a divine song.)

Thus rejected, the poet can find no earthly home. He is an exile; his origin is divine. Great poets from Homer to André Chénier have all known what it is to suffer, to be mistreated, and to be misunderstood. "All these great exiles from heaven," Banville says in "La Vie et la Mort," were crushed by life through poverty, hunger, or insults. Their only consolation was death, radiant death, which tenderly washed their wounds and spread out for them as a reward, earned but not received in life, a red carpet of victory and crowned them with a laurel wreath.

The poet as he is presented in Les Cariatides is not a social reformer in any specific sense. Banville calls him a porte-lumière ("a bearer of light"), but his light is from a higher sphere. He is not a democrat in the sense that he accepts the values of the majority. One of his important attributes, on the contrary, is that his values are so uncompromising, permitting no dilution, no lowering to invite popular approval. As an extension of this idea, the poet's task is not to display his intimate feelings before the public but to make shine before it the torch of eternal beauty. Long before Leconte de Lisle's vehement denunciation, in the well-known poem "Les Montreurs," of the prostitution of the poet's art through attempts to win popular favor by means of a shameless display of personal emotions Banville formulated a similar idea in "Pourquoi courtisane":

Pourquoi, blond poète,
Ouvrir au passant
Ta douleur muette,
Ta douleur muette,
Lys éblouissante
Que la foule jette
Et brise en passant?
(v. 5, p. 204)

(Why, fair poet, open up to the passerby your mute suffering, your mute suffering, dazzling lily which the crowd throws away and breaks as it passes?)

A Heterogeneous Collection

One of the most striking features of Les Cariatides is its great variety, especially in tone and form, a mark of the amazing versatility and even virtuosity of the young Banville. In addition to the alexandrine and the eight-syllable verse we also find the ten-syllable verse and not infrequently even poems written in verses of five or seven syllables, anticipating the taste of Paul Verlaine for vers impairs. Various strophic forms are to be found also as well as poems of fixed form whose origins date from medieval times or the Renaissance. Banville also experiments with rhymes, putting together, for instance, three *rimes plates* in the poem "Même en deuil."

This variety of expression is not usually arbitrary but rather fits the subject. "La Voie lactée," the longest poem in the collection, is serious in tone throughout. Written in alexandrines, it maintains a certain solemnity in harmony with its didactic pretensions, and at times comes close to being pompous, wordy, and overloaded with names and other details. Some relatively long poems such as "Les Baisers de pierre" are narrative in character. Here Banville's tone is less solemn. In some of them he adopts Musset's *causerie familière*, taking the reader into his confidence and intervening personally on occasion. The eight-syllable verse can often be found in other serious poems whose character is nondidactic and lyric rather than narrative. Very often Banville uses short verses and short stanzas when the tone is light and the subject is less serious. "Loys" has the tonality of a Romantic ballad based on medieval material, reminiscent of Hugo's "La Fiancée du timbalier." "Leïla," while not really a pantoum, reminds us of one with its two parallel melodies. In "Les Caprices" Banville offers twenty-four *dizains*, poems of ten verses, each verse consisting of ten syllables. In them he maintains a playful lightness after the manner of Clément Marot. The rondeaux, triolets, and madrigals that compose "En habit zinzolin" are all addressed to some nymph or maiden from legend or mythology. Thus Banville appropriately borrows his material from the past to suit these old forms.

Earlier I observed that it is difficult to discern what is original in Banville's first collection of poems. The great variety of techniques complicates a problem already rendered difficult by the abundance of the poet's imitations and borrowings. Yet his particular stamp gradually emerges and there are indications here and there of his personal view of the world. The central fact for him is that he is a poet and as such he cannot see life through the eyes of a politician, a sociologist, or perhaps even a novelist. Although his conception of the poet is not radically different from that of many Romantics, he does not hold the view that the poet is a reformer and prophet. This is only to say that his ideas in this respect are close to those of some of his contemporaries, such as Gautier and Baudelaire. A more important point here is, not what he thinks the poet is or should be, but simply the fact that he makes of the poet and poetry the central subject of his writing.

From the standpoint of style Banville's personal contribution in Les Cariatides is a certain lightness of manner, which willy-nilly invades even those poems of more serious intent. Grace, ease, and elegance are general attributes of his poetry as early as Les Cariatides. He handles the familiar chatting style without difficulty and is a master in the art of breezy statement and personal intervention. In one of the dizains of "Les Caprices," for example, he gives a brief history of French poetry, first by telling of its richness before the seventeenth century, and then by formulating Malherbe's reactionary role in the following way: "Tant qu'à la fin pour mettre le holà / Malherbe vint, et que la Poésie / En la voyant arriver s'en alla" (v. 5, p. 253) (So much so, that in order to put a stop to it Malherbe came and Poetry, seeing him arrive, went away). In the last dizain he tells the reader that, having now written his twenty-four dizains, he wants to get away from the bourgeois for a whole day and read some of Gautier's poems. From time to time we sense a burlesque vein in him, the need to express his humor and to amuse himself (and perhaps us). Even in a serious poem such as "Le Pressoir" he cannot resist his penchant for punning. Who, reading the last two verses, can help thinking of Frère Jean des Entommeures's Rabelaisian pun on "divin" and "du vin": "Qu'importe, si pour tous, au bruit d'un chant divin, / Ruisselle éblouissant le flot sacré du vin! (v. 5, p. 235).

Finally, what appears unique to me in Les Cariatides is Banville's visible poetic world. It is an unusual amalgam of Greek mythology, contemporary Paris, and Watteau landscapes complete with stock characters from the Commedia dell'Arte. Fairies and nymphs are as real to him as the Parisian bourgeois. His world seems often to be like a fête galante, the atmosphere of which he evokes with consummate skill well before Verlaine, its dreamy and wistful figures, melancholy yet charming, bathed in soft and sad moonlight.

The appearance of Les Cariatides brought critical reaction in a very short time. Some could not believe that this was the work of an eighteen-year-old; Gautier, in fact, made the error of stating that the author was twenty-one. Both Gautier and Baudelaire, while noting the heterogeneous character of the collection and the difficulty of identifying the poet's originality, came to the conclusion that the book's most noticeable characteristic was its lyricism (4). The austere Alfred de Vigny, to whom Banville had given a copy, called on the young poet the same evening and by the next day had read and annotated all its poems, expressing in his comments understanding and encouragement. The critic Jules Janin wrote Banville a four-page letter containing both praise and criticism and asking for an explanation of his "audaces romantiques." Verlaine reportedly found _Les Cariatides_ more gripping than the "condensation and basic austerity" of Baudelaire's _Les Fleurs du mal_ (5). Perhaps the general reaction of Banville's generation is best summed up by Max Fuchs: "Romantics at heart, sufficiently cultivated to like the learned and artistic poetry of the sixteenth century, classical on occasion to stop the bourgeois from being classical, and fanciful in order to have the right to dupe them, hostile toward a shopkeeping and money-grabbing royalty, but too purely artistic to pass over freely to militant literature, such were the young men who applauded the appearance of _Les Cariatides_ (6).

Banville was now being noticed. Victor Hugo opened up his salon to him, a supreme honor for the young poet. In addition he was beginning to meet more writers in connection with several journals, such as _Le Corsaire_ and _La Patrie_. He was still living with his parents, who had moved to rue Monsieur-le-Prince. Here in a magnificently decorated room but with almost no furniture Théodore himself began to give receptions.

Chapter Three

The Funambulist

Les Cariatides marked only the beginning of a rather productive career for Banville. In the span of fifty years he produced seventeen collections of verse spaced at fairly even intervals between 1850 and 1880. In discussing Les Cariatides I indicated two visages of the poet, which could be linked in the broadest sense perhaps with the comic and tragic masks. Banville himself seems to identify two kinds of poets in his studies of Pierre de Ronsard and Jean de La Fontaine, both of whom he admired greatly (1). Ronsard, he says, will never be a popular poet in France because of his triumphal, noble, proud, and ornate manner. The public is hostile to this imperious role of a poet who identifies himself with the gods and is conscious of his high mission. La Fontaine, on the other hand, possesses the gift of comedy and appeals even to those who say they dislike poetry. Readers identify with him, with a certain spirit of apparent innocence or naiveté under the protection of which he can dupe and dominate through his shrewd mockery those masters whom on the surface he seems to obey.

Perhaps it can be argued that most poets are composites of these two tendencies. But in Banville they are unusually clear-cut and he is aware of them. Indeed it is difficult to say which of these visages dominates over all. In some of his poetry he is a clown, a verbal acrobat, a prosodic virtuoso, a satirist, or a light-hearted singer; at other times his voice is that of the divine soul of man exiled on earth, singing the sufferings of all exiles and recalling visions of lost paradise. The two currents are sometimes intermingled, but frequently they are well separated. The collection that most completely incorporates the first of these approaches, which could be termed the funambulist spirit, is his Odes Funambulesques of 1857. The second tendency finds its best expression in Les Exilés of 1867. These two collections are thus central in his poetry. Most of the others are related to one or the other of these two and with them form two more or less distinct groups. It is on this grouping that I propose to base my discussion of most of his poetry, recognizing that some of the choices for the two groups may be arbitrary on account of their participation in both tendencies.

Les Stalactites

Just four years after Les Cariatides Banville published his second book of poems, Les Stalactites. This title, like the first one, suggests sculptured, hard forms. If we take the title together with the opening and closing poem, we can find in them some of the basic ideas of a Parnassian art poètique. "Dans les grottes sans fin brillent les stalactites" (In the endless caves the stalactites glisten) is the opening line of the first poem, "Décor." What follows is a veritable feast for the eyes, the evocation of exotic scenes constituting an almost surrealistic vision of disparate objects reminiscent of the colorful and imaginative inventions of Hugo's Les Orientales. No sense of anachronism is felt in the combination of exotic gardens, the Moorish Alhambra, fairy-tale cities, sphinxes, griffons, monstrous gods in clowns' costumes, basilicas, diamond towers of Babel, and nymphs. But the creation of this rich array of color and shapes, this rare and flamboyant setting suggested by the stalactites, has required "the tears of evenings and of dawns," and "these divine caprices are frozen tears." Thus in a sense the stalactites suggest the poetic process, human emotion captured and held in a durable form. The closing poem, addressed to the sculptor, is an exhortation to choose carefully a marble without flaws, "en attendant l'extase" (while waiting for inspiration). It then asks the sculptor to produce a perfect vase. The emphasis is on the hardness of the material and above all on the purity and perfection of the finished product.

The visual, pictorial, and sculptural emphasis conveyed by these two poems, however, applies only minimally to the rest of the poems in the collection. If perfection and purity of form mean mastery of technique for Banville, then these two poems can be said to be consistent with the spirit of the collection, for technique and especially rhythms constitute its chief preoccupation. But, rather than a Parnassian concern with physical objects, Banville's approach is more characteristic of the Symbolists in his experimentation with rhythmic forms and his fascination with half tones and suggestive vagueness. Whatever their views may be about the separation of form and content, I think most readers would agree that it is much more difficult to extract content from Les Stalactites than from Les Cariatides. The poems of the former are shorter, on the whole less wordy and declamatory, and more polished.

In his preface Banville expresses the hope that readers will notice that he has changed his style, introducing a "certain softness." The preface begins with his characterization of modern man: "To regain lost joy, to climb again with fearless steps the azure ladder that leads to heaven, such is the incessant aspiration of modern man, who no longer feels himself to be condemned or enslaved, and who from day to day understands better the necessity of believing in his own virtue and in the immeasurable love of God for his creatures" (2). If he has celebrated Beauty, Strength, and Love by their Greek names, he says, it is because it falls to lyric poetry eternally to precede human philosophy "like the dawn." The rest of the preface reads like a manifesto of Symbolist poetry, beginning with a defense of half tones: "In fact it would not be any more sensible to exclude half light from poetry that it would be reasonable to wish it absent from nature; and it is necessary to have recourse to the artifices of negligence in order to leave certain poetic objects in a twilight that envelopes them and in the atmosphere that bathes them. It is art that teaches how to disdain art; it is the rules of art that teach how to abandon rules." The need of this approach, he adds, is felt especially "when it is necessary to express in poetry a certain order of sensations and feelings that could be called musical."

Although Banville gives no further indications concerning these sensations and felings, he alerts the reader to a number of songs and imitations of popular rounds contained in Les Stalactites in preparation for a later book to be called Chansons sur des airs connus [Songs on familiar airs], a book which he never completed.

One reason for Banville's preoccupation with rhythm

is that for him it is linked with the pulse at the very heart of the universe, with the mysterious and inner essence of life itself. This view is suggested in "L'Ame de la Lyre" and "A Olympio." Both poems incorporate the myth of Prometheus, a myth somewhat foreign to Banville's nonrebellious temperament, but which he adopts here from Victor Hugo, especially in "A Olympio." In this poem, addressed to Hugo, as its title might suggest, the poet is seen as a rival of God, determined to possess the secrets of the universe. Like Prometheus, he will be a stealer of fire:

> J'irai jusques au ciel, dans ses voûtes
>   profondes,
>   Lui voler pour mes vers
> Le rhythme qu'en dansant chantent en choeur les
>   mondes
>   Qui forment l'univers.
> Je boirai le nectar de la force première,
>   Et dans la main du dieu,
> Impassible titan, chercheur de la lumière,
>   J'irai voler le feu.
>
> (v. 2, p. 93)

> (I shall go right to the sky, into the depths of its vaults, to steal from it for my verses the rhythms which the worlds forming the universe sing in chorus as they dance. I shall drink the nectar of primordial forces, and in the hands of the god, impassive titan, searcher after light, I shall go to steal fire.)

His creation will be comparable to that of God, giving life to lowly clay.

"L'Ame de la Lyre" bears an epigraph from George Sand: "Daughter of man, I am a part of the spirit of God. This Lyre is my body." The image of the lyre is combined with the myth of Prometheus. It is he who gives the lyre its soul by letting it have a spark of that divine fire he has stolen. Although Banville does not make the comparison explicit, the poem appears to suggest a parallel between the human body and the lyre, both containing that divine spark which is the soul. This soul, remembering distantly its divine origin, is conscious of its imprisonment and aspires to escape from "the cold prison of meters and verses" and ascend to heaven in order to hear the perfect rhythms of the voices of "the choir of the universe."

The important point is, not that Banville borrows a Platonic idea or repeats the Romantic conception of the poet as a Prometheus figure, emulator and rival of God, creating as God created, but that these poems provide a philosophical foundation for Banville's emphasis on rhythm and song. He is not so much concerned with expressing thoughts as he is with song. In a sense he is an experimenter in techniques of versification. In _Les Cariatides_ the rondeaux, triolets, and madrigals, together with the _dizains_ after the manner of Marot, already pointed in this direction. In _Les Stalactites_ the practice of restoring many of these older forms, especially popular songs with studied rhythms, is more prevalent. The number of poems whose titles begin with the word _chanson_ ("song") is striking. Banville is inspired here, not by Hugo and Musset, but by Heinrich Heine and Ronsard.

The imprint of Ronsard and the Pléiade is especially noticeable. One of the best-known poems of the collection is probably "A la Font-Georges," which Sainte-Beuve admired. It is preceded curiously enough by an epigraph from Boileau, a poet whom Banville ridicules on several occasions and whose uncomplimentary references to Ronsard are well known. Its beginning is unforgettable and establishes the general tone and flavor of the whole poem:

> O champs pleins de silence,
> Où mon heureuse enfance
> Avait des jours encor
> Tout filés d'or!
> (v. 2, p. 43)

(Oh fields full of silence, where my happy childhood had days that were still all spun out of gold!)

In this poem evoking the happiness of childhood Banville has borrowed the rhythmic pattern of Ronsard's "Ode de l'élection de son sépulcre," which is admirably suited to the intimate and modest utterance of Banville (3). Another poem, "Carmen," celebrating the beauty of Camille, is reminiscent of Ronsard's "Quand vous serez bien vieille. . . ," in the complicated and sinuous movement of its quatrains with their long sentences composed of numerous clauses and members introduced by participles. "A une petite chanteuse de la rue" adopts a stanzaic form composed of verses of three and seven syllables used by Ronsard in "Le bel aubépin" and by Rémi Belleau in "Avril." It appears especially suitable to communicate the wistful mood of the speaker, whose reflections about the origins of the girl with the guitar evoke several landscapes, ranging from the Rhine with its banks overgrown with vineyards to Sorrento with its "blond shores," and lead him to imagine that she might be an incarnation of Mignon, Little Red Riding Hood, or Columbine. This last figure plunges him into the dreamy world of a Watteau painting, leaving him to wonder about the whereabouts of Columbine, Harlequin, and Pierrot. The refrain of "La dernière pensée de Weber" follows another form known to the Pléiade, similar to that of "A une petite chanteuse de la rue" but with the three-syllable verse dominating.

It is not difficult to find other examples of technical experimentation. "Sonnet sur une Dame blonde," suggesting a comparison between the lady and the beauty of an evening sky, is written in tetrasyllabic verse, a most unusual choice for a sonnet (but even sonnets in monosyllabic verse exist in French literature!). "Le Triomphe de Bacchos" employs the extremely rare thirteen-syllable verse rather effectively to evoke the ostentatious and orgiastic procession of Bacchus and his followers. In "Ronde sentimentale," which might be said to anticipate Leconte de Lisle's "Les Elfes," Banville experiments with decasyllabic verse by putting the cesura after the fifth syllable instead of the fourth as was customary. He innovates in rhyme as well. In "Elégie," for example, he breaks with the time-honored practice of alternating masculine and feminine rhymes. What he does is to produce rhymes between masculine and feminine syllables throughout the poem, as illustrated by the two opening verses: "Tombez dans mon coeur, souvenirs confus, / Du haut des branches touffues!" (v. 2, p. 71) (Fall into my heart, mingled memories, from the height of the dense branches!).

In some instances ("Ronde sentimentale," "Nous

n'irons plus au bois") Banville takes popular refrains as his starting point and attempts to assemble "like the pearls of a necklace, impressions and emotions, not independent, of the same type doubtless, but without logical connection" (4). The large number of poems with refrains is striking but not surprising in view of Banville's overriding concern with songs and rhythms suitable for songs. But he sees rhythm also in a glass of wine, as in "Chanson à boire": "Je vois dans le flacon vermeil / Couleur de lune et de soleil / Des rhythmes danser en musique" (v. 2, p. 20) (In the red flagon the color of the moon and of the sun, I see rhythms dancing in music). In "La Symphonie de la neige," dated five years before Gautier's "Symphonie en blanc majeur," Banville wants to demonstrate that music can exist as harmonious relationships and to record the plaintive rhythm of "toutes les blancheurs" (all the whitenesses) which the snow inspires and calls forth out of past dreams. Angels, clouds, swans shivering in lakes, the foam from which Aphrodite rose, and many others--these all lend their voice and their rhythm to create this symphony.

Although the collection is dedicated to Banville's father it contains only one poem addressed to him. This and the ode to La Font-Georges are the only purely personal poems in the book. The tone of Les Stalactites is almost nowhere somber. Even when the poet approaches the subject of death in "Dans le vieux cimetière. . ." he inspires no feeling of morbid pessimism. The cemetery is a "place of delight," the dead "must be happy," and nature bathing this sublime decay of human bodies with its rays lovingly transforms them into beautiful flowers. His love poems generally have a fresh and joyful flavor. Their mood is not the romantic melancholy of autumn or of the dying day, nor do most of them express the urgency of living related to the awareness of the brevity of life. They simply celebrate the joys and beauty of love and living.

Banville's emphasis on music, his abundant use of vers impairs or asymmetrical verse, his preference for muted tones and suggestion of moods lend to Les Stalactites a certain casual grace. His careful mastery of technique allows him to achieve an effect of unstudied ease, "Sans rien en lui qui pèse ou qui pose" (Without anything in it that might be heavy or ponderous), to quote a line from Paul Verlaine's "Art poétique."

The *Odelettes*

The next few years were not entirely happy for Banville. Ironically, his father died the very year when *Les Stalactites*, dedicated to him, appeared. By 1850 the poet's health was beginning to deteriorate and he narrowly escaped death from illness in 1852. Still his writing continued. Whereas *Les Cariatides* had been regarded as the work of a precocious adolescent, *Les Stalactites* was taken somewhat more seriously but without creating any major stir in the literary world. His circle of friends and contacts in the realm of art and literature was widening, partly because his collaboration on the staffs of various journals facilitated numerous contacts of this kind. He had begun his journalistic work with *La Silhouette* in 1845. Three years later he was with *Le Pamphlet* and from there he went in rapid succession to *Le Corsaire* and *Le Pouvoir* (later known as *Le Dix Décembre*). During the early years of the Second Empire he was with *Le Paris*, *La Revue de Paris*, and *Le Figaro*. His production of verse continued in a fairly regular manner. Late in 1853 some of his new poems began appearing in *Le Paris*, and in 1856 a collection of poems from the years 1846 to 1856 was published under the title *Odelettes*.

At the head of the collection stands a dedication to Sainte-Beuve, who is addressed as *cher maître* ("dear master"). Banville pays warm tribute to him for having rediscovered Ronsard and the "France des rimeurs d'odelettes." He praises Sainte-Beuve's criticism in which he has "blended the most rare nuances of personal feeling in a form molded by a craftsman's hand." He calls Sainte-Beuve's entire work the *odelette* of the nineteenth century and acknowledges the debt he owes to this great poet-critic from whose *Pensées de Joseph Delorme* and *Notes et Sonnets* following the *Pensées d'août* he has learned so much. It is in this spirit of gratitude that he now offers these *Odelettes* like "clusters of wild grapes from his harvest" (5). The preface that follows the dedication explains the choice of title by attempting to define "odelette": it is an "ode-epistle sentence, a type of familiar speech elevated and disciplined by the lyric cadences of a short and precise rhythm. It is, if you like, a drop of essence of rose sealed beneath a narrow agate in the setting of a ring, a birthday present, a daily reminder of fleeting joy" or a waltz or mazurka theme commemorating a moment of affection or love (6). He then proceeds to give a short sketch of the history of the genre: born in Greece, it made its first appearance in France with Charles d'Orléans and reached its greatest distinction in the sixteenth century with the Pléiade and Philippe Desportes, subsequently falling into disfavor.

In the sense that Banville wishes to recapture the echo of some of these songs from the past and to employ abandoned rhythms, this collection is related to _Les Stalactites_ and is a continuation of similar preoccupations, again to a considerable extent technical. In fact, the _Revue de Paris_, directed at the time by Louis Ulbach and Maxime du Camp, immediately attacked the _Odelettes_ for its lack of content, while admiring its technical mastery (7).

The _Odelettes_ of 1856 consists of just over two dozen poems, almost all short. Their rhythmic forms are strikingly varied. A distinct preference for shorter verses can be noted, the alexandrine being used in only two poems. The lyricism of the collection is characterized by an apparent simplicity and a good-natured, almost casual air. The impression of casualness comes, not from the use of everyday vocabulary and not from neglect or carelessness, but rather from conscious and careful craftsmanship, art that conceals art. Purity is Banville's first concern. A small unpretentious subject is almost a necessity; the dimension of the precious stone must not be allowed to detract from its setting. The setting, however, will put the stone in relief and isolate its purity. Here is how Banville expresses his aim: "An _odelette_ does not last any longer than the trill of a nightingale, but for the play of these trills and these arpeggios quickly flown away a voice of constantly pure timbre would be required" (8).

As in Banville's first two collections, personal poetry is rare. Perhaps there is only one poem that really belongs in this category, and that is "A Zélie," recalling the happy childhood days the poet spent with his sister and, like Lamartine's "Milly," visiting each part of the family property in turn and evoking its beauty and the memories connected with it. He recalls also the premature death of their grandmother and echoes questions asked in Lamartine's "Le Lac": "Ma soeur, ma soeur, n'est-il pas de défense / Contre l'affront du temps? / Qui les a pris, ces jours de notre enfance. . . ?" (v. 2, p. 126) (My sister, my sister, is there no defense against the assault of time? Who has taken them, the days of our childhood?).

Nostalgic melancholy, however, is not a dominant mood in the collection. Rather its atmosphere is festive. While recognizing the brevity and fragility of life and love, Banville celebrates the joys of living. In "A Jules de Prémaray" he exclaims, "C'est vous seuls qui vivrez toujours, / Printemps, lauriers, chansons, étoiles!" (v. 2, p. 172) (It is you alone who will live forever, spring, laurels, songs, stars!). The opening poem "Loisir" sets the tone. It is May, winter is over, and the trees are in leaf and in bloom. It is time to enjoy the mood of spring, to think of love, to forget serious concerns, and to indulge our dreams. And so, while violets are spreading their perfume, the poet says, he will rhyme some _odelettes_. Wisdom consists in loving wine, beauty, and springtime; all the rest is vain, and when our body lies in the grave, what remains? The poet's reply, in "A Adolphe Gaiffe," might have been supplied by Musset: "D'avoir aimé / Pendant deux ou trois mois de mai" (v. 2, p. 138) (To have loved for two or three months of May). Serious-minded dreamers tell us that we should seek causes and effects. "Just words, just words," the closing line tells us. "Let us gather roses." "Chant séculaire" evokes the coming of a golden age in which all the values the poet prizes will be realized: devotion, liberty, and genius will all flourish; art will be unveiled like a starry sky; and, evil having been vanquished, beauty will be resplendent over the earth.

Although Banville presents several portraits of beautiful women and celebrates love, the woman to whom he is most attracted is the Muse, and through her he exalts poetry and song. It is striking how many of the _odelettes_ are addressed to poets and other artists. In "A Sainte-Beuve" the portrait of the Muse is more accurately an incarnation of rhyme. The opening stanza pictures a beautiful lady, richly clad, standing at the door of a Renaissance chateau looking over the green hillside. This opening tableau is more than vaguely reminiscent of the last part of Nerval's "Fantaisie," which incidentally is also classed as an odelette. The completed portrait shows her as a composite of beauty and grace on the one hand, and strength and authority on the other. She is identified as rhyme, "delight and torment of our life," to be loved and obeyed. The poem closes with these lines: "Tu le sais bien, toi qui, tout jeune, / As été son plus cher amant!" (v. 2, p. 115) (You well know this, you who when very young were her dearest lover!). The reference of these two verses is clear when we recall that Sainte-Beuve almost three decades earlier had published a poem entitled "A la rime," in which he calls rhyme the "sole harmony of verse" and acknowledges its primacy in the poetic process.

Another French poet Banville admired was Théophile Gautier, whom he regarded more as a master than as a colleague. What student of French literature is not acquainted with Gautier's "L'Art"? But perhaps it is worth recalling that this poem, first published in L'Artiste in September, 1857, under the title "A Théodore de Banville," is a reply to Banville's odelette "A Théophile Gautier," dated May, 1856. This circumstance explains Gautier's opening word "Oui" as an expression of his agreement with the contents of Banville's poem, which he then restates and develops further, using the same verse form and even echoing some of the expressions used in the odelette. For example, "Pas de travail commode" becomes "Fi du rythme commode" in Gautier's poem. It is ironical that, although this time Banville is not the imitator, it is the imitation that is more generally known to readers. There are subtle differences between the two: Banville's poem is less developed and it gives relatively less importance to the idea of hardness of material and more to the poet's vision, to which he refers as "his pure caprice," "the idea with a serene brow," the state of ecstatic madness, and the dream as a wild bird.

Another poem that needs to be singled out is "A Méry." Here for the first time Banville represents the condition of the poet through the image of the funambulist and anticipates "Le Saut du tremplin," a major poem in his Odes Funambulesques. The first half of "A Méry" evokes the skillful performance of the famous funambulist Madame Saqui, precariously placed between two abysses, between the heavenly heights and the pavement below. "Tel est le sort du poète" (Such is the poet's fate), Banville declares. He is a tightrope walker destined to suffer:

> Dans l'azur aérien
> Qui le sollicite, ou bien
> Sur la terre nue et froide
> Qu'il aperçoit par lambeau,
> Il voit partout son tombeau
> Du haut de la corde roide, . . .
> (v. 2, p. 132)

(In the airy azure which calls him or on the bare and cold earth which he perceives in fragments, he sees everywhere his tomb from the height of the taut cord.)

The precariousness of the poet's position and the difficulty of maintaining lasting equilibrium are underlined by the asymmetric seven-syllable verse, too fluid to permit any sensation of solidity, and by the long sentences and rhythmic groups that allow few pauses and leave few opportunities for the relaxation of tension.

The *Odelettes* foreshadow the *Odes Funambulesques* in several ways in addition to the conception of the poet as a tightrope walker. This is accomplished partly through references to the contemporary scene. More than half of the poems are addressed to Banville's contemporaries (Houssaye, Sainte-Beuve, Asselineau, Murger, the Goncourts, Karr, Gatayes, Méry, Gavarni, Gaiffe, Lebarbier, Boyer, Gautier, Grange, Prémaray). Some of these poems take as their starting point some current event or situation while others refer to the ordinary prosaic life of every day. Banville shows a growing awareness of the bourgeois as the dominant class in his time and of the conflict of values between it and the poet.

Another way in which the *odelettes* prepare the *Odes Funambulesques* is by their tone. Like *Les Stalactites*, they are generally light, but I think there is a subtle difference at times in the introduction of something approaching satire and in a certain facetiousness of expression. In "A Roger de Beauvoir," for instance, the poet holds up to good-natured ridicule the seriousness of the bourgeois, who disdain such joys as wine, love, and beauty and lead a colorless life overemphasizing the value of thrift. Through the use of the foreign term "speech" and a comparison with bulls he suggests that they are pompous and perhaps stupid:

> Et les bourgeois que flatte
> Un speech verbeux
> Ont peur de l'écarlate
> Comme les boeufs!
> (v. 2, p. 155)

(And the bourgeois flattered by a wordy speech fear scarlet like bulls!)

He calls them "these merchants," "morose people," and worst of all "people without flame who through a sense of duty clothe even their souls in a dark suit." "A un riche" once again contrasts two sets of values. To the rich man who can afford satins and whose drawing room is luxuriously appointed he says, "Ma foi, vous avez bien raison / . . . / de ne pas célébrer Phyllis / En odelettes" (v. 2, p. 148) (My word, you are certainly right not to celebrate Phyllis in *odelettes*). He can afford to speak in prose, but the poet, supping on moonlight, also has riches in his world made of rhyme. Two extremes of expression occur in the poem as if to embody the two contrasting levels of wealth. To evoke the luxurious living quarters of the rich man Banville employs an ornate circumlocution stating that this man can see the "arrows of Apollo fall into the gold" of his drawing room. On the other hand, he as the poet employs at times familiar, conversational language with an occasional parenthetical aside, such as "je frissonne d'y penser" (I tremble to think about it). But the very fact that he uses this familiar tone in addressing the rich man, as for example the "Ma foi" at the beginning, turns out to be a type of satirical weapon which says in effect: I do not respect you enough to address you in more careful language.

The *Odes Funambulesques*

In February, 1857, hard on the heels of the *Odelettes*, appeared what many regard as one of Banville's most important books of verse, the *Odes Funambulesques*, a title with which his name has come to be linked. Many of the poems, the earliest of which dates from 1844, had previously appeared in *La Silhouette* and a few in other journals such as Le Pamphlet, Paris, Le Mousquetaire, Le Corsaire, and Le Figaro. Most of them were anonymous. In the preface to the first edition Banville states that they did not deserve to be signed, while in a later preface he explains that the author's signature did not belong with them because he was only seeking a new form and had not tried "to create a manifestation of his thought" (9). According to his commentary he had not even planned to collect these poems in a volume, but when a friend asked him when his "odes funambulesques" would appear, he decided then and there to collect and publish them under that title (10).

That this volume made an impression on the reading public is clear. It overshadowed what he had written previously, and for some readers even today Banville is known primarily as the author of the Odes Funambulesques. It established his reputation as a juggler with words for whom poetry was a game totally lacking in ideas and feeling. Its mischievous playfulness and buffoonery are unmistakable, and its general mood has been admirably captured in the first stanza of a poem addressed to him by his contempory Auguste Vacquerie:

> Ton volume éclate de rire,
> Mais le beau rayonne à travers.
> J'aime ce carnaval du vers
> Où l'Ode se masque en satire. (11)

(Your volume rings with laughter but beauty shines through it. I like this carnival of verse in which the ode wears the mask of satire.)

Banville is not usually regarded as a satirist, or at least not as a great satirist. His Odes Funambulesques contain many references to life in his day, but he has failed to endow them with that universality without which satire cannot be great and lasting. Too many of the objects of his buffoonery are meaningless today. Who, for example, would know that L'Ombre d'Eric is a novel by Paulin Limayrac? Who has heard of François Ducuing, Xavier Dunière, or Doctor Véron? And who is aware that Louise Colet for a time signed her work Louise Colet, née Révoil? Yet such knowledge would be necessary to appreciate fully Banville's allusions. As early as 1873, his publishers, sensing that the reading public was already finding many of his references obscure, asked him to add a commentary explaining them.

Was it Banville's intention, in the first place, to be a satirist? The answer is not simple. On the one hand, it is clear that he did not regard himself as a social or political reformer. During his life he was to witness a number of important political events: the overthrow of the July Monarchy, the Revolution of 1848, the founding of the Second Republic, the *coup d'état* of 1851, the war of 1870, and the fall of the Second Empire. In spite of the republican tradition of his family and the fact that he collaborated most often on journals of an anti-imperial bias, his attitude toward the Second Empire tended to be moderate. For one thing he was indebted to it for aiding him financially during his illness when he received expensive treatment from Dr. Louis Fleury at Bellevue. Still his political convictions do not seem to have been well defined. In recalling that, at the outbreak of the Franco-Prussian War, his friend Charles Asselineau was accused of being a Communard, he exclaims: "Great Scott, he who in the realm of politics had the same ideas as I, that is to say, no ideas at all, and limited himself to belonging to the Romantics!" (12). Nor did Banville have any illusions about the *Odes* as an instrument of reform, declaring in his preface, "They will in no way change the face of society. . ." (v. 1, p. 5).

But the central question for Banville relates to the bourgeoisie. He grew up at a time when among artists, especially after 1830, there was a general resentment of the bourgeoisie. Many of the younger artists manifested their hatred of the "philistines" in practical jokes, shock tactics, mystification, and fantasy to oppose the so-called practical sense of the bourgeois. Banville's contempt for the bourgeoisie was not so much a question of economics or of political ideology but of artistic and moral values. On this point he makes his stand quite clear: "I share with the men of 1830 an inveterate and irreconcilable hatred of what was then called *le bourgeois*, a word which must not be taken in its political and historical meaning and as signifying the third estate; for in Romantic terms, *bourgeois* meant a man who has no other cult but that of the hundred *sous* coin, no other ideal except the preservation of his own skin, and who in poetry likes sentimental romance and in the plastic arts colored prints" (v. 1, p. 294).

The victim of Banville's jokes is most often the bourgeois, who represents for him mediocrity, materialism, the commonplace, smug self-satisfaction, and accepted ideas as opposed to original thought and sincerity. The bourgeois mentality as he identifies it knows no boundaries of occupation or social status. Politicians, financiers, shopkeepers, and men about town can all be bourgeois. Even some writers, such as Eugene Scribe to whom Banville invariably refers as Monsieur Scribe, can belong to this class. He even manages to group the prostitute in this category, although he accords her a somewhat more sympathetic treatment, recognizing that in her cynicism she tends to be more honest than the ordinary bourgeois and sometimes more pretty.

Perhaps the key to understanding Banville's funambulist spirit is as much his view of literature as his attitude toward society. It has to do with his conception of the poet as a funambulist. The basic condition of the poet is to be a martyr. That is an honor, the only one the poet has no right to refuse. Some outstanding men have attempted to escape this martyrdom, but they all had a witty or comic side to them, and even so their attempts to avoid suffering have led to "long distressing silence and personal pain" (13). For Banville the most notable example of a poet of this type was Heinrich Heine, whom he regards as the greatest poet of the century after Victor Hugo. He considers Heine "the most modern of men," the poet who has found "the only way of depicting a civilized and complex era," which is to unite "wit and inspiration." _Atta Troll_ represents for Banville the model of the modern poem, the fusion of the modern and the ancient, of Christ and Apollo. Heine is "Apollo and Aristophanes, comical and lyrical at the same time," possessing "song and irony, the caress of love and the cutting whip" (14). Not only is the comic approach a partial shield for the poet suffering from the mediocrity of reality, but it is a more accurate means of mirroring modern life, which in those aspects that can be observed is "essentially absurd and caricatural" (v. 1, p. 15).

The role of the modern poet is the subject of "La Corde roide" and "Le Saut du tremplin," the opening and closing poems of the _Odes Funambulesques_. These poems take up and develop further the ideas of the odelette "A Méry." "La Corde roide" notes the fall of the poet from his Orphic state. Now his voice is drowned out by the sounds of the roulette wheel and the bank. He is tired of preaching love to the rock and gentleness to the tiger. How can he reach men? What disguise will permit him to address them? The mocking mask and the laughter of irony will perhaps allow him to voice his protest in favor of the gods now rejected. But whatever mask he takes, whatever means he chooses, he will steadfastly refuse to lower his values: "Il marche sur les fiers sommets / Ou sur la corde ignoble, mais / Au-dessus des fronts de la foule" (v. 1, p. 24) (He walks on proud summits or on the ignoble rope, but above the foreheads of the masses). Thus the poem introduces the image of the tightrope walker in accordance with the title of the collection, and it justifies the funambulist approach as a means whereby the poet may be noticed. He may not be heeded, but at least he will have been true to himself in raising his voice on behalf of the gods.

"Le Saut du tremplin" might very well have been incorporated in Banville's "exile" poems were it not for the fact that the central figure is a clown on a springboard. In his commentary Banville states that he has tried to express the attraction of the "gouffre d'en haut" (the abyss on high), adding that he also likes to end a book with the word étoiles ("stars"), which also ends Dante's Divine Comedy (v. 1, p. 385). He achieves the latter ambition by picturing the clown springing so high that he bursts through the ceiling of the circus tent and ascends into the heavens to roll among the stars. This unlikely event underlines the idea that it is equally unlikely for the poet to realize his lofty ideals in this life. The clown-poet is consumed by his thirst for the purity of "that lapis whose azure covers our moving prison." There is nothing comical about him. He is no longer interested in puns, and even though his public applauds, he wants to rise toward the "gouffre d'en haut":

Plus loin! Plus haut! je vois encor
Des boursiers à lunettes d'or,
Des critiques, des demoiselles
Et des réalistes en feu.

Plus haut! plus loin! de l'air! du bleu!
Des ailes! des ailes! des ailes!
(v. 1, p. 290)

(Farther! higher! I can still see speculators with gold-rimmed glasses, critics, girls, and fired-up realists. Higher! farther! some air! some blue sky! some wings! some wings!)

Nothing short of the rarified upper sphere will do. Bourgeois mediocrity oppresses him, and his impatience to break with it is conveyed partly by the broken rhythms of the last two verses, suggesting the flapping of wings symbolizing ascent.

If the dull gray of uniform mediocrity made Banville's era intolerable for him, his greatest challenge, as perhaps for the Flaubert of Madame Bovary and L'Éducation sentimentale, was to confront "la Banalité et la Platitude," which he terms in his commentary "the most frightening of all monsters," and to cast upon them the golden light of morning "which gilds everything it finds in its way, including melon peels and old slippers" (v. 1, p. 348). Accepting the idea that in his complex age everything is heightened in intensity, Banville tries to depict its spirit through exaggeration and caricature. Having donned the costume of the clown, he gives the whole collection a certain carnival atmosphere, which may remind us of Hugo's parody in Les Châtiments of Louis Napoleon's regime presented as a vulgar circus. But Banville's touch is much lighter than Hugo's and the caricatural nature of his satire diffuses any sense of bitterness or hatred (15).

Few would disagree with those critics who noted a poverty of ideas in the Odes Funambulesques. Nor would Banville have contested that judgment. His stated aim was to create a new form. Whatever satire and whatever image of nineteenth-century France these poems contain, they owe to a large extent to their form and technique. What Banville regards as the novelty of his approach has to do with versification. Having studied Molière, Rabelais, Racine's Les Plaideurs, and other comic literature, he imagines a "new versified language of comedy appropriate to our life and to our contemporary poetry, and which would come out of the true nature of French versification by seeking in rhyme itself its principal means of comedy" (v. 1, p. 2).

For him comedy, satire, and parody must remain poetry. As in lyric poetry, the particular effect produced, in this instance comedy, "is always obtained by combinations of rhyme, by harmonic effects, and by particular sonorities" (v. 1, p. 330). To achieve this end Banville sees the necessity of liberating traditional verse from some of its constraints, making it more supple and more airy in order to remove some of the obstacles to comic effects. As he says in his witty and colorful manner, "it is impossible to remain fiery on a placid horse" (v. 1, p. 17). By making rhyme the dominating principle he emphasizes the verse as a unit and imposes a certain symmetry on the most familiar, prosaic, or even absurd comments, and the rhyme itself frequently requires a word to complete it which common sense could never admit but which the reader readily accepts as a metric necessity.

The collection is made up of seven groups of poems: *Gaîtés*, *Évohé*, *Folies nouvelles*, *Autres Guitares*, *Rondeaux*, *Triolets*, and *Variations lyriques*. *Autres Guitares* is the central part, the odes proper. *Gaîtés* can be regarded as an introductory section, whose chief function seems to be to establish a circus or carnival setting. Titles such as "La Corde roide" and "Mascarades" speak for themselves. The former, as we have seen, introduces the image of the tightrope walker. "Mascarades" invites the Muse to celebrate the carnival and evokes its sights and sounds. A festive spirit pervades *Gaîtés*. Paris itself is adorned like a bride, and with its sidewalk cafés, passersby in shirtsleeves, pretty girls, and lilacs in bloom, its mood is one of joyful celebration. But the last verse of "Premier Soleil" tells us there are exceptions:

> C'est le temps où l'on mène une jeune maîtresse
> Cueillir la violette avec ses petits doigts
> Et toute créature a le coeur plein d'ivresse,
> Excepté les pervers et les marchands de bois.
> (v. 1, p. 48)

> (It is the time when one takes one's young mistress to pick violets with her small fingers, and every creature's heart is full of intoxication, except that of the perverse and the wood merchants.)

Here we can see an example of Banville's use of rhyme

as a means of satire. The key word is "bois." The whole verse which it completes is manifestly dissonant within the context of the poem. Yet we willingly accept "bois" as a necessary sound to rhyme with "doigts." Its presence creates associations and contrasts. The wood merchants are a special group within the general category of merchants, and merchants are representative of bourgeois materialistic society. Here they are linked with the "pervers" and in a sense are guilty by association. In contrast with the hearts full of the joy of living, in the next to last verse, the word "bois" suggests dryness, lack of any feeling in these merchants. Finally, the opposition suggested between "marchands de bois" and "ses petits doigts" evokes a certain coarseness contrasting with the daintiness of the fingers that touch and pluck the violets.

Évohé, which follows *Gaîtés*, consists of six poems introducing some of Banville's grievances against his age and calling upon the Muse to sound the trumpet and prepare the whip of satire to combat and expose the enemies of poetry, the degeneration of music, the exploitation of children, prostitution, and the general degradation of love. Again the bourgeois bear the blame. In "Académie royale de musique," for instance, the speaker, wishing to go to the opera, ends up at some cheap bourgeois meeting place with vulgar displays of wealth. He thinks the coachman must have lost his way. But no, a conversation with some of the guests reveals that this is really the opera. Its standards are unbelievably low: the violins sound unpleasant, the orchestra is too loud and not in tune, the chorus is disorganized, and the changes of stage scenery are always missed. The performance reminds him of a review of the civic guard. Banville's skill in the use of sound is again demonstrated in *Évohé*. As an example, here is a passage from "Les Théâtres d'enfants," expressing the general depravity of morals:

> Nulle part, fût-ce même au fond de la Cité,
> L'Impudeur, la Débauche et la Lubricité,
> La Luxure au front blanc creusé de cicatrices,
> Et le Libertinage avec ses mille vices,
> Ne dansèrent en choeur ballets plus triomphants!
> C'est ce que l'on appelle un *Théâtre d'enfants*.
> (v. 1, p. 66)

(Nowhere, not even in the core of the city, did Immodesty, Debauchery, and Lubricity, Lust with its white forehead furrowed with scars, and Libertinism with its thousand vices dance in chorus more triumphant ballets! That is what is called a children's theater.)

Apart from the richness of the end rhymes, the passage weaves a dense texture of assonance and alliteration echoing the key rhyme of "Cité" and "Lubricité," especially in the repetitions of _l_, _u_, _c_, and _i_.

After _Les Folies nouvelles_, an amusing interlude whose atmosphere resembles that of Watteau's _Fêtes galantes_ combined with elements of Italian comedy and of Shakespeare's world of Oberon and Ariel, we come to _Autres Guitares_, whose title is borrowed from Hugo's "Autre Guitare" in _Les Rayons et les Ombres_. In his commentary Banville states that "these are poems rigorously written in the form of odes" (v. 1, p. 331). He goes on to explain that he has made extensive use of parody of Hugo and indicates the poems he has used as models. Why has he done this? Others have parodied Hugo, but through ideas only (v. 1, p. 333). Banville wants to show that he can achieve his poetic ends not so much through ideas but essentially through music, for the music of the verse can, by the quality that is proper to it, awaken everything it wishes in our mind and create even that divine and supernatural thing, laughter (v. 1, p. 333)! Most of the poems in _Autres Guitares_ concentrate, not on satirizing society nor even faults of individuals, but rather they make individuals appear ridiculous often for no apparent reason. Of the twelve odes in this section about two-thirds are parodies of poems by Hugo. Some follow their models very closely while in others only a distant resemblance is discernible. One of the best examples of Banville's technique of parody is "V.... le baigneur," imitating Hugo's "Sara la baigneuse" from _Les Orientales_ (16). Both poems present bathers. For the exotic and beautiful Sara, Banville substitutes the paunchy Doctor Véron. Hugo's stanzaic and verse forms, borrowed from Ronsard, are retained and very few changes are made. Here are the opening stanzas of the two poems:

(Hugo)	(Banville)
Sara, belle d'indolence,	V...., tout plein d'insolence
Se balance	Se balance
Dans un hamac, au-dessus	Aussi ventru qu'un tonneau
Du bassin d'une fontaine	Au-dessus d'un bain de siège,
Toute pleine	O Barège,
D'eau puisée à l'Illyssus;	Plein jusqu'au bord de ton eau!
	(v. 1, p. 144)

"Indolence" becomes "insolence" and the basin of the fountain is replaced by a tub of water. An amusing wordplay furnished by the rhyme of tonneau ("barrel") and ton eau ("your water") suggests the barrel-shaped body of Véron sitting in his bath water, and perhaps awakens other comical associations in the reader. Two stanzas later we find the following parallel:

On voit sur l'eau qui s'agite	On voit de l'eau qui l'évite
Sortir vite	Sortir vite
Son beau pied et son beau col.	Son pied bot et son faux col.

Here the image is completely transformed by a minimum of changes. In Hugo's poem we see Sara's pretty foot and neck above the surface of the water. In Banville's version the substitution of a different preposition and of one letter in the first verse, together with three slight changes in the third, produce an enormous transformation in the image. The bather is so ugly that the water shuns him, and what we see protruding from the bath is his club foot and his detachable collar. In the next stanza Banville creates an absurdly funny situation:

Reste ici caché, demeure!
Dans une heure,
Comme le chasseur cornu
En écartant la liane
Vit Diane,
Tu verras V.... tout nu!
(v. 1, p. 145)

The suggestion that anyone would like to see this man naked, as the faun waited to see Diana naked, is utterly ridiculous. The introduction of mythology in this prosaic context is incongruous, but it is skillfully achieved through the rhyme of cornu ("horned") and nu ("nude"), which not only links the faun with

V...., but also suggests the possibility of some similarity between them.

Autres Guitares and the last three sections, Rondeaux, Triolets, and Variations lyriques, contain an abundance of verbal acrobatics, including unusual enjambements, rich rhymes, puns, assonances, and other groupings of sounds. In "L'Ombre d'Eric," which is also the title of a novel by Paulin Limayrac, Banville parodies romance in general but he also punishes Limayrac for his criticism of some great writers, by making him appear ridiculous through the repetition of the verse "Si Limayrac devenait fleur" (If Limayrac were to become a flower), occurring at the beginning and end of each stanza. In "La Tristesse d'Oscar" Banville amuses himself (and his contemporaries) by repeating the word "collet" and linking it with "Révoil": "Plus de collet d'aucune sorte, / Aucun collet, pas même un collet. . . né Révoil. . ." (v. 1, p. 149). These two verses cannot be translated into English without losing their point, which was that for Banville's literary contemporaries "collet" immediately suggested "Révoil" because the poetess Louise Colet used to sign her poems by adding "née Révoil" to her name. In "Le Flan de l'Odéon," a satire of mediocre versifiers writing for various journals and of the jealousies and intrigues in these circles, an enjambement is amusing by itself: "C'était le doux Napoléon / Citrouillard, l'un de nos vieux maîtres . . ." (v. 1, p. 158) (It was the gentle Napoleon Citrouillard, one of our old masters). The incongruousness of the man's two names is aptly underlined by the separation effected through enjambement. As if that is not enough buffoonery, Banville has him choose an actress by the name of Asphodèle Carabas as editor of Le Tintamarre, where she translates Anacreon "En vers de quatre centimètres" (in verses of four centimeters).

It is not difficult to understand why Banville chose such forms as rondeaux and triolets when we consider that by their very nature they require certain repetitions either as rhymes or as refrains. The rondeau, requiring a refrain consisting of the first word or two of the poem and added after the second and third stanzas, lends itself especially to punning. This allows Banville in "Mademoiselle Page," for example, to employ the word "page" three times, meaning "page" as in a book, "page" in the sense of attendant, and "Page" as a proper name. Sometimes Banville is attracted by the sheer pleasure of combining sounds, without any concern about whether any meaning accompanies them. He is fascinated, for instance, by the combination of the names of three actors that always appeared in the same order on billboards. They were Néraut, Tassin, and Grédelu, and to them collectively or individually he devotes five triolets. He becomes a veritable juggler playing with the name "Néraut" in the triolet by that title:

> Les rôles ont tous un air haut
> Quand ils sont joués par Néraut.
> A Nérac, Néraut, en héraut,
> Fut pareil à Néro dans Rome.
> (v. 1, p. 214)

To accumulate further examples would serve no useful purpose. In a short poem added in 1873 as an epilogue to the *Odes* he states that his book contains no bitterness, no baseness. Although his purpose was not to reform society, he has left his imprint on it through the integrity of his art. One of the remarkable aspects of his achievement is that in the confrontation between the mediocrity he saw in his day and the high standards of his own artistic vision, the latter have remained intact.

The *Occidentales*

In many ways the *Occidentales*, published in 1869, may be regarded as a continuation of the *Odes Funambulesques*. In his dedication to Pierre Véron, editor of *Le Charivari*, Banville states that, having demonstrated in the *Odes Funambulesques* the immense potential for comedy that the French language can exploit in its union with the lyrical element, he had decided not to go farther in that direction. However, he has yielded to a request to write some odes for the weekly *Figaro* and he has not been able to refuse Véron's charming request for more odes. Consequently, in 1868 he wrote most of the odes making up the *Occidentales*, publishing many of them the same year in *Le Charivari*. The following year they appeared in a volume under the title *Nouvelles Odes Funambulesques*, which in the second edition, in 1875, was changed to Occidentales, an obvious parody of Victor Hugo's Les Orientales.

Although Banville's general approach in this volume is similar to that of the Odes Funambulesques, the tone is not as light, his criticisms are more biting, and to his already impressive arsenal of comical effects he has added further techniques. He now points to more specific imperfections of contemporary France and especially Paris: the general mediocrity, dullness, and bad taste of the bourgeois; inferior theater, art, and music; the hypocrisy and political meddling of the church; the erosion of freedom; excessive government spending; militarism and war; the sacrifice of the beauties of parts of Paris to Baron Hausmann's urban modernization; loss of religious faith; prostitution; the display of the female body in various stages of undress on stage; and the incompetence of the French Academy.

If Banville is not likely to be remembered as a great satirist, it is his virtuosity as a poet that can still arouse our interest in the Occidentales. A half dozen or more of these poems attack the imperfections of his age globally, introducing very nearly the same list of criticisms. But it is remarkable that each one employs a different technique. "Soyons carrés," as the first example, depends heavily on sarcasm. After exposing the ills of the time, the speaker advises that things be left as they are, for as Voltaire affirms, "Tout est bien comme il est" (everything is fine as it is)! Another technique he uses is that of changing the perspective. "A Vol d'oiseau" illustrates this: two men in a balloon see the globe from a distance now, and the substance of their conversation about the earth is that they must have been wrong in thinking it was imperfect, since from this vantage point no defects are visible. By implication the distant viewpoint is in error and the accuracy of the original one is reinforced.

A new perspective can come also from a change in state rather than distance, as is the case in "Ancien Pierrot." Pierrot, having committed an indiscretion with the fairy Azurine, is punished by being turned into a man. She assures him that he will have to suffer man's fate only until the evils of earthly human life will have been removed. Even though he cannot see signs of improvement he is reassured in his naive way, thinking that all will be well. But in the reader the opposite conviction is reinforced.

"Et Tartuffe?" illustrates another approach. Here the biblical Adam and the literary Tartuffe in alternating quatrains evoke the opposing states of paradise and of modern France. Each quatrain representing the latter is introduced by the question "Et Tartuffe?" recalling the familiar scene in Molière's play which presents parallel reports on the illness of Elmire and the robust health of Tartuffe. The answers contained in the quatrains make up an accumulation of vices, so that Tartuffe's name is linked with suppression of freedom, quarrelsome polemics, disdain of beauty, licentiousness, thirst for violence and revenge, hatred, envy, and stupidity.

In a facetious vein Banville in "Trop de cigarettes" attributes France's troubles to cigarette smoking. Taking as a starting point the fact that Emperor Louis Napoleon smokes, he concedes that if his age is sometimes off course, "c'est la faute du cigare" (it is the cigar's fault). But he wishes to take a closer look at modern Paris by the light of its lantern, "roi de la Liberté" (king of liberty). He explains his play on words by adding in parentheses the word "journal." Then follows a whole inventory of criticisms, ending with this amusing conclusion:

Je pense alors sous mon tilleul
Songeant à nos peines secrètes,
Que l'Empereur n'est pas le seul
Qui fume trop de cigarettes!
(v. 3, p. 118)

(Then I think beneath my linden tree, reflecting on our secret troubles, that the Emperor is not the only one who is smoking too many cigarettes.)

Banville's taste for hyperbole is evident in the Occidentales as it is in the Odes Funambulesques. In the poem "Delirium tremens" all nuances, all relativism, are absent. All values are reversed and the absurd becomes the norm: "heads" means "tails"; the prostitute criticizes the morals of other women and complains that she is being violated; traitors cry treason; and thieves cry thief. There is a danger that God may be damned and the devil canonized. Even Rothschild may die of hunger. Obviously Banville's statements are so exaggerated as to be absurd themselves, and instead of gripping satire we have amusing comedy.

In attacking growing militarism, armaments, and war, he employs exaggeration in both directions, overstatement and understatement. The rifle invented by Chassepot is condemned several times. In "Satan en colère" Banville imagines Satan crying for mercy because, since Chassepot's invention, the number of clients he is receiving is so great that he can no longer accommodate them all in his fiery cauldron. "Le Siècle à aiguille" envisions a future in which progress will manifest itself in a state where there will be nothing but soldiers. "O bonheur inconnu" (Oh unknown happiness), he comments sarcastically, adding the comically absurd image of the butcher and the cloth merchant both using a naked sword to cut their merchandise. In "La Balle explosible" he evokes the gruesome, bloodthirsty nature of the goddess of war, who feasts on the sight of bodies from which blood gushes and entrails protrude, and who derives pleasure from having her horse trample men underfoot. The clip-clop of the horse's hoofs echoes in the verse, "Et l'homme, et l'homme, et l'homme, et l'homme!"

"La Mitrailleuse" provides one of the best examples of Banville's euphemistic expression. The poem opens with three quatrains describing in an ironic tone all the charms of the machine guns with their _jolis petits canons_ (pretty little barrels). And just like an organ, this weapon, "to charm our eyes," is operated by turning a crank. This lightness of comment to treat a subject of great seriousness is reminiscent of Voltaire's technique in evoking the horrors of war in _Candide_, for example. The continuation of the poem also parallels Voltaire's manner of combining gruesomely realistic detail with light and euphemistic statement. The grim irony that results cannot but make one shudder:

> Grâce à quoi dragons verts, cuirassiers,
> fusiliers,
> Déchus de leur beauté physique,
> Tous, par douzaines, par centaines, par
> milliers,
> Seront foudroyés en musique.

Un enfant y suffit; alors, dans un éclair,
Notre chair sous le plomb féroce
Volera par lambeaux ensanglantés, sur l'air
Allez-vous-en, gens de la Noce!
(v. 3, p. 110)

(Thanks to which green dragoons, cuirassiers, fusiliers, fallen from their physical beauty, all, by dozens, by hundreds, by thousands, will be struck down to music. A child can do it; then, in a flash, our flesh beneath the fierce lead will fly in bloody shreds to the tune of Allez-vous-en, gens de la Noce.)

A comic effect akin to burlesque sometimes results from the contrary technique of employing solemn language and a serious tone with trivial subject matter. This occurs, for example, in "Tristesse de Darimon." A splendid ball is about to take place at the Tuleries. Darimon, who, the poem tells us, became famous for his culotte courte ("short pants"), is not invited. Thereupon he addresses to his culotte a solemn ode, which we can immediately recognize as a parody of Hugo's "Tristesse d'Olympio." Out and out buffoonery is especially present in the first quatrain, where the disparity between the elevated tone and the less-than-elegant subject matter on the one hand, and the incongruous association between the latter and Apollo on the other, create an image so ridiculous that laughter can be the only response:

--O culotte! lambeau de ma joie envolée!
Toi qui naguère, ici montagne, ailleurs vallon,
Ainsi qu'un gant docile à ma jambe collée,
Moulas avec orgueil des formes d'Apollon!
(v. 3, p. 52)

(Oh pants! shred of my joy flown away! Thou who but lately, here a mountain, elsewhere a valley, like an obedient glove clinging to my leg, didst mold with pride the contours of Apollo!)

Banville's rich technical and stylistic resources are further illustrated in "Le Petit-Crevé," a portrait of a kind of useless fop. His outstanding characteristic is that he is not really alive:

> Plus endormi qu'une citerne,
> Il végète. Faux col géant.
> Favoris courts. Veston. L'oeil terne.
> Signes particuliers: Néant!
> (v. 3, p. 72)

(More asleep than a cistern, he vegetates. Enormous detachable collar. Short sideburns. Coat. Dull eyes. Distinguishing features: Nothing!)

In this quatrain there is only one verb, "végète," a verb that expresses lack of activity. The telegraphic style with its lack of verbs underlines the absence of action in the fop's life, and the broken rhythm parallels the fragmented nature of his existence. He knows nothing of human values such as beauty, honor, virtue, patriotism, or liberty. And when he dies, Banville concludes, no one will be able to notice that anything has changed in him.

It should not be forgotten, of course, that Banville's basic aim was to produce comedy through versification. This he continues to do in the Occidentales. His enjambements are especially bold. In "Embellissements" enjambement occurs four times after a preposition, once after a definite article, once between an auxiliary verb and its past participle, and twice after the word "rue" in the name "rue de la Paix." This means that the definite article, the prepositions, and the word "rue" become rhyme words. They have been torn away from the words with which they normally form a unit, and in this way the poet creates a verbal parallel to the demolition and renovation of the rue de la Paix, which is the subject of the poem.

Banville's rhymes are often ultra-rich. Occasionally we are reminded of the Grands Rhétoriqueurs, as for example in this rime à écho from "Soyons carrés": "Que Ponson de Terrail sous la muraille raille. . ." In the same poem we find this tour de force of rhyme and assonance:

> Que Legouvé, sublime et fier, lime sa rime!
> Que sans nul intérim
> Le bon Petit Journal, toujours minime, imprime
> Quelle frime de Trimm!
> (v. 3, p. 23)

(Let Legouvé, sublime and proud, file his rhyme. Let the Petit Journal, without interim, always minimal, print some hoax by Trimm.)

In the context the repetition of the i vowel may very well emphasize the smallness of the literary efforts in question, but it is difficult to resist the impression that such combinations of sound contain a substantial gratuitous element as well, providing a certain type of amusement independent of other meaning.

The Trente-Six Ballades joyeuses and Rondels

If the Odes Funambulesques and the Occidentales form the heart of Banville's funambulist poetry, his Trente-Six Ballades joyeuses and his Rondels are at its periphery. In both of these collections his chief interest is the rehabilitation of old verse forms. They are manifestations of his obsession with rhythmic patterns. A poet must "possess all known rhythms and if necessary create others," we read in one of his short stories (17). Both the medieval ballade and the rondel, with the technical difficulties built into their fixed forms, challenge the poet's virtuosity and allow him to display his verbal acrobatics.

The first of these two collections was composed between 1861 and 1869. Dedicated to the memory of Albert Glatigny, it bears on its title page the notation that the ballades have been composed in the manner of François Villon. In a short preface Banville states that the ballade is one of the most essentially French of poetic forms. Its characteristics are "clarity, joy, a singing and rapid harmony," and it is "easy to read and difficult to make" (18). He further contends that whoever employs a poetic form from another time or idiom must accept all its traditions including the choice of subject. At the same time, to guard against sterility, the poet must breathe into it the soul of his age. To promote a better understanding of the ballade form, he then includes a short history of the ballade by his friend Charles Asselineau, who maintains that in the late Middle Ages the ballade reached its greatest distinction, characterized by complete freedom of subject and tone, its only prescription being rhythmic.

To a considerable extent Banville succeeds in his announced intention to copy the manner of Villon and also to infuse the ballade with a modern spirit. The image he projects of himself in "Ballade sur lui-même" is calculated to remind us of the artlessness of Villon. He, Banville, is a mere "assembleur de rimes," a child of nature, shunning the servile activities of the city and knowing only versification ("Je ne m'entends qu'à la métrique"). His ballade in honor of the Virgin not only refers to Villon's ballade, but the beginning of its refrain, "Dame des cieux," echoes the opening of Villon's poem, "Dame du ciel." The flavor of Villon's time is sometimes produced through the use of such archaic terms as "onc" for "jamais" or by the omission of articles, a common practice in medieval French. Like Villon, he remembers those who have been closest to him, notably his mother, whom he assures that, having been born "pour le rhythme et pour la poésie," he will take as his law "to sing correctly in various meters."

But Banville was more richly blessed with family than Villon. In 1863 he had met a widow named Marie-Elisabeth Rochegrosse, whom he married three years later. He treated her little son Georges as his own, and altogether the life of this little family appears to have been unusually serene and happy. To both wife and son he devotes a ballade. His "Ballade à sa femme, Lorraine" extols his wife's many domestic virtues. The fact that she was born in Lorraine, near Domrémy, establishes an association with the medieval heroine Joan of Arc and thus not only gives the ballade a vaguely medieval color but confers a nineteenth-century saintliness on his wife.

In spite of the many ways these ballades recall Villon, the spirit that animates them is not his. His haunting sense of sin and decay is almost totally absent. Perhaps Banville's penchant for hyperbole and his generally sunny outlook on life bring many of his ballades closer to the spirit of Rabelais. "C'est Rabelais qui nous verse du vin" (It is Rabelais who pours us wine) is the refrain of the "Ballade de la sainte Buverie." But the spirit of Banville's time, or at least his perception of it, is also present, and in this sense the volume is a continuation of the Occidentales. He regrets the year 1830, when the terminology of the stock market was still "Hebrew" to such great poets as Musset, Hugo, and Vigny; but now the sacred delight of poetry is threatened by materialism ("Ballade de ses regrets"). These are disdainful times, he says in "Ballade de Victor Hugo père de tous les rimeurs." Inferior and popular writing abounds. There are some superior writers like Gautier and Leconte de Lisle, but the haunting refrain recognizes the exiled Hugo as the father of poets: "Mais le père est là-bas, dans l'île" (But the father is over there on the island). In "Double Ballade pour les bonnes Gens" the refrain "Dieu fasse aux bons miséricorde" (God grant mercy to the good people) is a prayer made necessary by the vices of society. Merely through the combination of rhyme words, such as "financier," "négocier," "huissier," "balbutier," "soucier," "boursier," and "acier," Banville is able to suggest the prosaic, materialistic, and insensitive nature of his times. Even the beauty of Parisian women is so contrived that he calls them "un article de Paris" ("Ballade pour les Parisiennes").

The slender volume entitled _Rondels_, first published in 1875, contains twenty-four rondels "composed in the manner of Charles d'Orléans, French poet and prince, father of Louis XII, uncle of Francis I." In his dedicatory message to Armand Silvestre, Banville states, "I am trying once again to resurrect, after the triolet and the ballade, one of our French rhythms, whose harmony and symmetry are charming." For him the experience is like discovering a box of lost jewels which "the fierce XVIIth century almost threw into the water. . ." (19). Banville's twenty-four rondels are indeed like polished jewels, like a symmetrical string of pearls. Pure in form, they observe every technical requirement of the rondel as practiced by Charles d'Orléans. The subject does not matter; any one will do. Daylight and darkness, the seasons, the four elements, the times of the day, fishing and hunting, beverages, the stars and the moon, metals and precious stones--these are the subjects Banville has chosen.

It is with such apparent ease and grace that Banville makes each subject conform to the exigencies of the rondel that the word that perhaps best characterizes this collection is charm. The choice of subject, instead of limiting the development of the poems, often seems to lead the poet's imagination in new and unexpected directions, perhaps even because of, rather than in spite of, the requirements of the form. "Le Feu" is one example. The reader might expect some kind of evocation of the warmth and light of the flame. But there is little reference to the fire itself. The word feu calls forth the rhyme word peu ("little"). The opening, "J'ai fait allumer un grand Feu" (I have had a large fire lit), progresses by the fourth verse to "Ce temps-ci m'intéresse peu" (These times are of little interest to me). By the time we reach the end of the poem we have the image of a man relaxing in solitude in front of a cozy fire and reading Rabelais to take him away from an age he dislikes to a more heroic one.

As we have noted before, Banville's virtuosity often manifests itself in the choice of rhyme words. In "Le Vin," for instance, vin rhymes in turn with divin, Sylvain, and devin; and through these associations the poem awakens images suggestive of divinity, mythology, and magic. There are other sources of charm as well. "La Lune" compares the moon to a frivolous woman and then provides the reader with a surprise in the form of an unexpected enjambement, as capricious as the lady herself: "Et souvent elle se met une / Nuée en manière de mante; . . ." (And often she puts on a cloud as a kind of mantle). In "Le Thé," somewhat suggestive of Théophile Gautier's "Chinoiserie," the charm comes from the communication of the daintiness of the china cup with its designs and colors, and the association of the ritual of tea with the English in the opening line, "Miss Ellen, versez-moi le Thé" (Miss Ellen, pour me the tea).

The Trente-Six Ballades joyeuses and the Rondels do not figure among the most important of Banville's collections, to be sure, but along with the Odes Funambulesques they have contributed to the notion that Banville was little more than a verbal acrobat almost totally devoid of thought or passion.

Chapter Four
The Exile
Le Sang de la Coupe

With Le Sang de la Coupe I begin an examination of a group of poems revealing another important visage of the poet, his more serious side, his vision of the human condition, his view of man as an exile, and his nostalgia for a better past. This is not to say that in this group of poems he has lost interest in formal experimentation. Nor is the funambulist vein with its comic perspective totally absent here. While recognizing the risk of arbitrariness I have nonetheless tried to group together those collections in which Banville's view of man as an exile seems generally to dominate.

Published in 1857, Le Sang de la Coupe was begun the year Les Stalactites appeared. It is composed of some thirty poems devoted to two main subjects, the poet and love. "L'Invincible," which opens the collection, is a key poem in that it introduces both of these themes and links them to the title. It begins with a Prometheus image: the heart, victim of love, is torn open by the beaks of vultures. But the lover does not complain; he willingly accepts the suffering of his heart. As the poem unfolds, the image of the cup of wine undergoes a number of transformations, not always logically coherent, but motivated by association and suggestion. In the second stanza the speaker drinks his tears (i.e., his grief) and sees in the wine the red blood of the grapes trampled by the Bacchantes. The following stanza furnishes an explicit comparison between the wine from the crushed grapes and the blood streaming from the broken heart of the lover. But in his invitation to his friends to drink he also establishes a connection with poetry, which gushes from the heart lacerated by love. A suggestion of sacredness is introduced in the next stanza through the word calice ("chalice"), presumably referring to the heart, which still preserves in its depths the memories of his love. Yet he does not want to see into these depths. In vain he tries to drown in divine wine "that living fire" which devours him. In a final transformation the cup becomes the ocean; and the wine the water from which rises Aphrodite.

Le Sang de la Coupe as a title, meaning "the blood of the cup," becomes a central image produced by combining two components taken from different terms of the basic comparison between the blood of the heart and the wine of the cup. Its connotations are numerous. The blood suggests the suffering of the lover and the poet, and perhaps of mankind in general. The wine of the chalice adds the Christian theme of Christ's suffering and sacrifice. As the title of a collection, the blood of the cup may also designate the contents of the heart poured out into a molded form. Whatever the particular connotations may be for individual readers, the first poem together with the title sets the tone and indicates the general nature of the collection.

Much of Le Sang de la Coupe is a celebration of the poet and poetry. It pays tribute to a number of poets whom Banville admires: Corneille, Molière, Heine, and Hugo. Some of the poems make statements about the function of poetry and evoke the condition of the poet. Perhaps "Les Souffrances de l'artiste" is the best representative of this group. The artist is here regarded as an eternal victim faced with the impossible task of satisfying his public:

> Va, tu peux y jeter les océans, poète,
> Sans étouffer ses cris et son rire moqueur.
> La curiosité de la foule inquiète,
> Voilà le nom du gouffre où tu vides ton coeur.
> (v. 6, p. 38)

(Go ahead, poet; you can throw the oceans into it without stifling its cries and its mocking laughter. The curiosity of the restless masses, that is the name of the abyss into which you empty your heart.)

Regardless of what prodigies he accomplishes--whether he finds a body for the infinite, brings to life figures of clay, conquers form and light, overcomes the fierceness of the tiger with love, makes beauty to be born Venus-like from the foamy sea, or resurrects the gods from their bloody gibbets--the response of the public is Après? ("So what?").

The artist is thus a martyr who sacrifices himself for humanity whose indifference makes him its victim.

Three images represent his condition. First, the word Après? is like a chain that enslaves him as Prometheus was chained to a rock. The second image is that of Christ: the poet suffers from the disdain of the passerby who will not even deign to touch the wounds made by the lance in His side and the nails in His feet. The last image, really a variation of the second one, is that of the pelican, familiar to many readers through Musset's "La Nuit de mai." The pelican is happy to die in the knowledge that its blood has left those he loves well nourished. But what anguish must the pelican feel if in death's agony his young were to say, "We are still hungry"? The suffering of the poet is not measured by his sacrifice but by the cruel awareness that his sacrifice is in vain.

While the concept of the suffering and self-sacrificing poet is already linked with the Romantics, the degree of insensitivity and indifference that Banville attributes to the public seems to me to be more characteristic of the post-Romantic period in France. Leconte de Lisle's solution (if it is one), stated in the familiar "Les Montreurs," is that he will not deliver the intimate secrets of his heart to an uncultivated and insensitive public. It is not difficult to think of other French writers of the period who reacted in a comparable fashion. Banville himself, inspired by the example of nature, offers similar advice in "A la forêt de Fontainebleau":

> Poëte, voile-toi pour le vulgaire vain!
> Qu'il ne puisse à ta Muse enlever la ceinture,
> Et souris-leur, pareil à la grande Nature!
> Sous ta sérénité cache aussi ton secret!
> (v. 6, pp. 98-99)

(Poet, put on a veil before the vain common herd. Let it not be able to take off the girdle of your Muse, and smile at them like great Nature. Beneath your serenity hide your secret also.)

In the last lines the poet asks the forest whether he has not made his soul and visage silent and gentle like a beautiful landscape. In the absence of a reply by the forest a reader could very well answer affirmatively, noting that even when Banville speaks of the greatest suffering of the poet, no great burning passion can be detected. In contrast to the unconcealed anger of Leconte de Lisle in "Les Montreurs" Banville's "A la forêt de Fontainebleau" is indeed "silent and gentle." His technique of "veiling" himself consists partly in offering us Banville the poet and refusing, with rare exceptions, to open up to us Banville the person. One of these exceptions in Le Sang de la Coupe is the charming "A la Font-Georges," evoking his childhood happiness with a gentle and touching simplicity reminiscent of Du Bellay's nostalgia for his birthplace, his "petit Liré," and even echoing that poet's "Quand reverrai-je..." with his own "Quand pourrai-je...."

Banville's view of the poet, however, is far from being totally somber. He sees in the poet an indivisible continuity. The poet belongs to the present "by the very fact of his existence; to the past, from which flows his inner life, by tradition and memory; and to the future, by his aspirations" (1). Something of this vision is incorporated in "Vous en qui je salue une nouvelle aurore...," a radiant poem, full of optimism for the future and feelings of fraternity among poets. He imagines himself seated next to Ronsard drinking nectar in the abode of poets, a kind of Valhalla, more Greek than Norse, and befitting gentler heroes. He is the link connecting the past, his master Ronsard, with the young poets of the future, whom he welcomes affectionately into the fraternity. The poem is filled with echoes of Ronsard's well-known sonnet "Quand vous serez bien vieille...." Ronsard will be beneath the ground resting in the shade of the myrtles; Banville's heart will sleep under the fruitful earth among the rose bushes. Both imagine how much their verses will be admired. Ronsard's "vous émerveillant" is echoed by Banville's "s'émerveille." Both have celebrated love and feminine beauty.

In "La Prophétie de Calchas" the sage Calchas admonishes his listeners not only to respect the Muses and the Lyre but also not to offend "winged Amor, king of the earth." Although he reserves a more exalted place for the Lyre, Banville may be willing to concede that love is the ruler of the earth. Le Sang de la Coupe shows us some of its faces. A number of poems celebrate feminine beauty. Banville is especially fascinated by long golden hair and by snowy breasts and nipples which he invariably compares to rosebuds.

The ambivalence of love, with its sensual pleasures but also its loneliness and unhappiness, is presented in the sonnet "La Nuit." Its opening is reminiscent of Baudelaire's "Recueillement" and to a lesser extent of his "Crépuscule de matin" in its evocation of the sleep of lovers sated from lovemaking. The second quatrain is heavy with sensual suggestion. The woman's hair is referred to as <u>flots extasiés</u> ("ecstatic waves"), the pillows are warm from her body, and the sheets kiss her breasts. The sestet communicates the loneliness, grief, and even despair that we sense here somehow to be connected with love. Banville succeeds in capturing something of the mystery of the night life of a large city, a rare accomplishment in his poetry, but one which gives "La Nuit" a distinctly Baudelairean flavor. Indeed, in his "Recueillement," published more than a decade after "La Nuit" was written, Baudelaire, who was a very close friend of Banville, may have recalled the opening of Banville's sestet:

> Vois-tu, du fond de l'ombre où pleurent tes pensées,
> Fuir les fantômes des pâles délaissées,
> Moins pâles de la mort que de leur désespoir?
> (v. 6, p. 56)

(Do you see, from the depths of the darkness where your thoughts are weeping, the ghosts of the pale abandoned women fleeing, less pale from death than from their despair?)

Banville recognizes the imperfections of earthly love and the disparity between it and his conception of ideal love. But love is part of the human condition. Man's accomplishments, however impressive, cannot change the fact that "the glory of Helen" will never be dispersed by time ("Homme, tu peux faucher..."). But if love will always remain as part of man's condition, so will mortality. "Tristesse au jardin" creates a portrait of a woman whose beauty is expressed in extravagant language. All of nature trembles with jealousy and shame. Each element of nature expresses its desire to die because it is less beautiful than she. But her reply shows the irony linked with her state: nature endures, while she, being human, and however great her beauty may be, must die.

In Le Sang de la Coupe Banville continues to experiment with poetic forms. In the preface he speaks of his efforts to find "a modern form" which he calls poëme (2). This would recognize the necessity of the poet to belong to the past, present, and future, and would in particular acknowledge the Hellenes as our real spiritual ancestors from whom has come our cult of beauty and heroism and whose religions harmonize with "our religion of forgiveness and love." The great writers of the seventeenth century sensed this spiritual kinship. Banville's conviction that this kinship "is the very soul of our poetry" is at the root of his long poem "Malédiction de Cypris," which he calls the most important of his attempts in the genre of the poëme. The central figure, Cypris, represents "the expansive force of life and of the renewal of beings," Banville explains. This long poem is at times disconcerting in its mingling of antiquity and nineteenth-century Paris. As the poem opens we see the Luxembourg Gardens with their "marbres de l'Attique" and their floral splendor on a beautiful June evening. The passing of soldiers seems vaguely linked with some outward show of heroism. Satyrs are stalking. The setting is suggestive of a kind of modern Eden sprinkled with figures from Greek mythology. Suddenly a golden chariot drawn by white birds descends in dazzling splendor, and in it is Cypris, reminding us vaguely of Diana with her large bow. She extols Paris, city of love, her temple and her altar, and reviews the names of famous women, painters, sculptors, and poets, which she has given to the city. She ends her eulogy with a hymn to love, "le seul vrai devoir et la seule science" (the only true duty and the only science), which has the power to make man like the gods.

Her speech completed, Cypris rises to a height from which she can observe the life of the whole city. A Homeric simile expresses the power and sweep of her vision:

> Telle du haut du ciel une aigle au bec vorace
> De mille oiseaux épars dans son vol suit la trace
> Et porte le carnage au milieu de leurs jeux;
> Telle, les yeux noyés dans les horizons bleus,
> L'héroïque Cypris d'un seul regard embrasse
> Le fond de la cité ceinte de mille feux.
>
> (v. 6, p. 22)

(As from the height of the sky an eagle with a voracious beak in its flight follows the path of a thousand birds and brings carnage into the midst of their play; so, her eyes lost in blue horizons, the heroic Cypris at a single glance embraces the depths of the city girdled with a thousand lights.)

At a glance she takes in the degeneration of Paris. Its very soul is summed up in the word "prostitution," prostitution of love, of art, of beauty, and of all values cherished by Cypris (and Banville). Sorrowful but angered also, she curses Paris in a long harangue with numerous subordinate clauses, introduced by Puisque ("since") and cataloguing its vices, dependent on the main verb Meurs ("die"). She predicts its eventual doom: "Ton heure vient..." (your hour is coming). The spiritual emptiness and sloth to which Parisians will descend before they finally realize their crime is effectively expressed in an image worthy of Baudelaire: "Mais quand le vaste Ennui, vieux comme l'univers, / Etendra devant toi son grand désert de sable / . . . / Tu te rappelleras ton crime haïssable" (v. 6, p. 35) (But when vast Boredom, as old as the universe, spreads out before you its great desert of sand . . . you will remember your hateful crime).

Her exit is as epic as her arrival was dramatic. All of nature trembles before her anger, and the poem closes with an evocation of the dawn expressed through an image of violence and destruction perhaps suggesting the demolition of the spiritual darkness of Paris and a promise of new light. While the poem contains individual passages of beauty, the inflated and declamatory language of much of it, against the background of bourgeois Paris, seems strangely incongruous and does not strengthen Banville's vision of close kinship between modern France and Greek antiquity.

Thinking more particularly of theater, Banville experiments with yet another form, created by the association of song and ode with dramatic dialogue, as the Greeks had done. What he has in mind, he explains in the preface, is the use of rhythms that are varied and linked according to the diversity of the situations and characters (3). An example of this approach, he adds, is "Le Jugement de Paris." This is the story of the golden apple left by the jealous Eris at the wedding of Thetis and Peleus, and intended for the most beautiful woman. Although the story is familiar, Banville attempts to treat it in a new way, as neither drama nor ode, but resembling both. There is dialogue but the speeches of the characters are cast in the elevated language of the ode. The two verses employed in most of the poem are the alexandrine and the octosyllabic verse. The chief function of the former seems to be narrative. When the chorus comments it usually employs a sprinkling of octosyllabic lines along with the alexandrines. The three goddesses in addressing Zeus alternate alexandrines with six-syllable verses whereas they speak to Paris in alexandrines. Speeches of a more lyric character tend to be written in octosyllabic verse, and Hermes, perhaps in conformity with his role as the swift messenger, also uses this rhythm. Thus Banville has tried to adapt rhythms to both characters and situations, and at least to the extent that he has created this combination of rhythms without noticeable artifice, his experiment can be termed a success.

"Le Jugement de Paris" can be regarded as successful in another way when considered in the literary context of the time. By 1846, which is the date Banville assigns to it, Leconte de Lisle had already written a number of his *Poèmes antiques*. The Parnassian return to Greek antiquity as a means of escaping from the hated contemporary scene or of recapturing notions of formal beauty was well under way. "Le Jugement de Paris" is a worthy representative in the large body of poetry inspired toward the middle of the nineteenth century by Greek antiquity. Its language is pure, dignified, and elevated; it is in impeccable taste, showing none of Banville's tendencies toward hyperbole or facetiousness; and the absence of any nineteenth-century reference preserves in it a feeling of distance which helps to give it a flavor of antiquity. Although much of *Le Sang de la Coupe* is in the Romantic tradition, as for example the notion of the suffering poet, it is in parts an expression of some of the trends later associated with the Parnassian poets. "Le Jugement de Paris" may be regarded as one of the most important poems of the collection to fit into that category.

All in all, *Le Sang de la Coupe* was not well received. Perhaps it was unfortunate that it originally came out as part of Banville's complete poetic works instead of appearing by itself. Perhaps also the fact that it was published shortly after the second edition of Leconte de Lisle's Poèmes antiques constituted bad timing and may have made Banville appear as an imitator. In a sense Banville's real position as a poet was still uncertain. Not completely a Romantic, he did not share the pessimistic attitude and erudition of some of the Parnassians.

Améthystes

Between April, 1860, and March, 1861, Banville composed a series of twelve love poems gathered together under the title Améthystes with the subtitle Nouvelles Odelettes amoureuses. He had gone to Nice to spend the winter of 1859 to 1860, hoping that its Mediterranean climate and his absence from the daily tensions of his journalistic duties might be salutary for him physically and psychologically. He was accompanied by the actress Marie Daubrun, over whom he and Baudelaire apparently had a disagreement, which fortunately for their friendship was of brief duration. While Marie Daubrun performed in Nice and Monaco and rehearsed much of the rest of the time, Banville was forced to spend much of his time in bed. Gradually, however, he regained some of his strength in the relaxed Mediterranean setting, whose waters touched on shores that had known nymphs and gods of a civilization that he admired so much. It was here that he composed two pieces celebrating France's annexation of the district of Nice and was awarded the Legion of Honor by the emperor.

The title page of Améthystes indicates a dedication to Marie, presumably meaning Marie Daubrun. It is possible that her inspiration figures prominently in the collection. But as is so often the case with Banville, his starting point appears based on formal considerations. The title is followed by the notation "composées sur des rhythmes de Ronsard." More particularly, he tries to revive combinations of masculine and feminine rhymes abandoned after Ronsard's time, when the alternation of masculine and feminine rhymes came to be regarded as obligatory. Banville follows no inflexible rule with respect to the arrangement of masculine and feminine rhymes in Améthystes. Some of the poems have only masculine rhymes; in others either masculine or feminine rhymes dominate; and still others observe the tradition of alternation.

"Les Baisers," the opening poem of Améthystes, gives us an indication of the flavor of the collection. Here is its opening stanza:

> Plus de fois, dans tes bras charmants
> Captif, j'ai béni mes prisons,
> Que le ciel n'a de diamants;
> Et pour tes noires trahisons
> J'ai versé plus de pleurs amers
> Que n'en tient le gouffre des mers.
> (v. 2, p. 195)

(The number of times when I have blessed my prisons, captive in your charming arms, exceeds the number of diamonds in the sky; and for your dark betrayals I have wept more bitter tears than are contained in the abyss of the oceans.)

The theme of the poem, and of the collection generally, is expressed in the first two verses. It is the paradox of love: the arms of the woman he loves are charming, but they hold him captive; he feels enslaved, but blesses his imprisonment. The firmness of the exclusively masculine rhymes tends to underline these bonds.

The essence of the collection as a whole is paradox. Not only is man a slave to love, not only does love inflict suffering and humiliation, but he accepts this condition without revolt, with a kind of serene resignation and even cowardly gratitude, ready to immortalize the woman through his art. Worst of all, he knows that he does all these things but cannot help himself. In this too he is an exile. Yet, strangely enough, Améthystes, in spite of this view of love, is not somber or depressing because to a large extent it is based on disparity between subject and form. Each of the twelve poems is like a polished jewel, graceful and elegant. The language, as in "Les Baisers," is often precious and hyperbolic. The short verse forms lend a certain lightness to the poems, again forming a contrast with the rather somber view of love. The longest verse employed, and that only rarely, is the decasyllabic one, while verses of eight, seven, six, and even four syllables are common. The exquisite "Nuit d'étoiles" and the charming "Le Rossignol," as examples, are written in verses of seven and six syllables respectively. The torn soul of the lover in the former poem and the sobs of desire and fright in the latter are submerged in the radiance of the night, in the beauty of the sea and sky, paralleling the beauty of the woman. The ambivalence of love finds an echo even in two rhymes, the masculine more sonorous and firm, the feminine softer and more gentle (4). Through form and language the poet triumphs over the wretchedness of the human condition he presents. Their beauty softens that wretchedness.

Les Exilés

The technique of clothing strong emotion or somber thought in a form whose beauty softens them or whose contrasting tone conceals them is not new. What intense passion lies beneath the polished beauty of Racine's alexandrines, for example! Of all the major poetic collections of his mature years Les Exilés, published in 1867, is the one in which Banville conceals least that suffering of which he regards poets as victims. That he himself had a special preference for this collection is clear from the opening of its 1874 preface: "This book is perhaps the one into which I have been able to put the most of myself and my soul, and if just one of my books were to remain, I would want it to be this one...." (5).

Banville calls the words of the title "ces deux mots d'une tristesse sans bornes" (these two words of an unlimited sadness). His own life in most of the decade preceding the publication of Les Exilés was also a time of sadness. Between 1850 and 1865 ill health plagued him, he was beset by financial problems, and he suffered from lack of recognition as a serious poet. He was saddened by the death of some of his friends: Musset, Brizeux, Marceline Desbordes-Valmore, Vigny, and Baudelaire. His life began to brighten in the last years before the collection was published. The 1860s saw the formation of the Parnasse contemporain, which helped to group together poets sharing certain ideas of poetry. Banville was able to enjoy a measure of recognition, at least for a brief time, as one of the central figures of the group. But probably the most significant event for him was his marriage in 1866, which gave him a happy home and the support of an unusual woman--Elisabeth Rochegrosse (6). As an accomplished hostess and good cook she played an important role in the receptions given by the Banvilles, first on the rue de Bucci and after 1875 on the rue de l'Eperon. She was wife, friend, nurse, and mother. The portrait that he has left of her in his Camées parisiens emphasizes her role as mother, not only to her small son, but also to him, "the useless rhymer who, through the very grace of the gift accorded him, will remain to his dying day an old child" (7). It is to her that he dedicates Les Exilés, in which he includes "A Élisabeth," a poem celebrating her virtues and expressing his love for her and his faith in a happy future together.

Of all Banville's collections of poetry I think Les Exilés is the most complete expression of his view of existence. The unifying thread of his vision is the idea of exile. Who are the exiles? To this important question Banville tries to supply at least some preliminary answers in his preface. The term is closely linked with sufferers and victims. There are victims of the tyranny of kings, but they are not the real exiles, for their country may allow them to return. Those exiled into poverty, vice, absence, grief, or pain are not the real exiles either, for they can be comforted and their emptiness filled "by repentance and the unbridled desire for heaven" (p. 6). The real exiles, Banville says, are those "infatuated with the beautiful and the just, who in the midst of men governed by base appetites feel burned by the divine flame and, wherever they may be, find themselves far from their homeland, worshippers of the dead gods, unyielding champions of defeated causes, searchers for a paradise covered with brambles and pebbles, and at whose gate even the flaming sword of the archangel, no longer needed, has been extinguished" (p. 7).

We see then that Banville appears to recognize greater and lesser degrees of exile, but the important fact is that for him the epic of man is the story of his exile. The concept of the epic of humanity as a collection of small epics, sometimes grouped in cycles, was widespread among nineteenth-century French poets. Perhaps the prototype of this genre was Hugo's La Légende des siècles, but many of the Parnassian poets attempted it too. Banville's Les Exilés is the collection that comes closest in his work to being a "legend of the centuries." It is a story of fall and redemption, but in a sense the reverse of the biblical version. In Les Exilés it is the gods who are driven off by man, and redemption is envisaged as the return of the gods made possible by the intervention of the poets. But man without the gods is an exile too, and thus man and gods are both exiles from the moment of the expulsion of the gods to the time of their redemption. The first poem of the collection relates their expulsion while the last one is devoted to their return and most of the intervening ones evoke various moments and aspects of man's exile.

The setting of the opening poem "L'Exil des Dieux" is Northern Gaul during the time of Emperor Constantine. The general atmosphere recalls such poems as Hugo's "La Conscience" and Leconte de Lisle's "Qaïn." The physical world is cold, gloomy, primitive, and empty. The monstrous oaks, huge dark clouds, and gigantic cliffs suggest a decor suitable for habitation by some pre-human race of primitive giants. All warmth has gone out of the world and even sunrise is presented through the image of violence. Nature is in mourning. The cliffs are tormented by sad thoughts, the cascades sob, and the ocean itself is in a state of grief. Suddenly a procession of gods appears, Olympians, walking soundlessly and ghostlike "toward exile, toward oblivion, toward the night." Expelled from Olympus, they have become subject to all man's sufferings and are now doomed to wander endlessly. The word "troupeaux" emphasizes their fallen state. In the divine made human there is a parallel between them and Christ, but they will be the redeemed, not the redeemers.

The Muses sing the despair of their exile. Aphrodite then speaks for the gods, first addressing the Titans. She acknowledges that the Olympians have chased the Titans "toward the abysses of Time," and calls upon them to witness that now man is expelling them, the Olympians. In this there is an echo of the idea, current in the nineteenth century, of a succession of creeds, each relevant for a time and then replaced by another until finally no gods are left. Aphrodite then turns to man. Her "Homme, vil meurtrier des Dieux, es-tu content?" (v. 7, p. 14) (Man, vile murderer of the gods, are you satisfied?) echoes Musset's words from "Rolla": "Dors-tu content, Voltaire...?" (Are you satisfied in your sleep, Voltaire?). She predicts that without the gods man's world will be empty and lifeless. He will become an exile, lonely and unknown. The gods will not be there to reveal his origins and his destination. Love and poetry will die and with them all that is divine in man. Only ugliness and suffering will be left for him. As the day breaks "in a sinister and somber twilight" the gods fade into the mist, and where Aphrodite's breasts of lilies and of roses had formerly left their radiant splendor, only a pale reflection of snow and fire remains, symbolical of destruction, of cold loneliness and consuming passions.

The opposite of the state of exile in the Banvillean sense might be regarded as universal harmony, as that unity of existence in which man and animals, nature and gods, all exist united by the bonds of some mysterious universal music. In "Le Berger" the poet communicates such an idea through the image of God the shepherd, whose flock consists of the heavenly bodies and who is at the same time like a conductor preserving the harmony of the universe. The disruption of this harmony brings exile and the chief manifestation of exile is isolation. One of the best descriptions of that state is given by Orpheus in "La Cithare":

> J'ai vu cela! j'ai vu que dans le firmament
> Comme ici-bas, souffrant du même isolement,
> Et séparés toujours par d'invincibles voiles,
> L'homme et les animaux, les Dieux et les Etoiles
> Vivaient en exil dans l'univers infini,
> Faute d'avoir trouvé le langage béni
> Qui peut associer ensemble tous les Etres...
> (v. 7, p. 65)

> (I saw that! I saw that in the firmament just as down here, suffering from the same isolation and still separated by impenetrable veils, man and animals, gods and stars, were living in exile in the infinite universe for failing to find the blessed language that can bind together all Beings.)

What should follow from Banville's premises is that man bears enormous guilt, for it is he who has brought about universal exile by expelling the gods. Banville does not stress this point, but he leaves no doubt about his conviction that man has fallen from divine origins. In "Le Berger" he may be thinking of the Positivism of his age when he speaks of those whose "hand believes in what it touches," and who say that God does not exist and heaven is empty. One important reason why Banville admires Greek civilization of antiquity is connected with the idea of exile. Time has tended to intensify man's exile, and man's memory of his divine origins has become dimmer. Not only do some men deny this heritage, but, worst of all, the question is often not even considered in a society whose chief concern is material gain. Small wonder then that earlier ages of human history seem so much more attractive to him, for in them man is temporally less distant from his divine beginnings. In particular, Banville sees in Greek mythology a measure of universal harmony in that its gods and heroes personify nature and have human attributes without ceasing to be divine. They are embodiments of that harmony.

Les Exilés, more than any of Banville's other works, presents a suffering world and reflects the poet's pity and sympathy for all suffering beings, beginning in "L'Exil des Dieux" with the Olympian gods who are subjected to pain, hunger, tears, old age, and all other ills known to man. In "La Cithare" Orpheus tells us of nature's suffering: the cliffs are chained to the earth, the waters of the rivers are forced into their channels, the trees are tormented by winds, and the waterfalls know loneliness. But nature has no voice to tell of its suffering and we remain indifferent to its plight. We disdain the animals, but when they are wounded they bleed just as we do. We humiliate them and even the gods turn away from them, Orpheus says.

Banville directs his attention especially to the suffering of man, whom Orpheus sees as a victim made of "glory and clay," "a being starved for love," whose happiness, if he finds any, is cut off in a brief moment by death. Man's suffering is inextricably linked with love. The god Amor in "La Fleur de Sang" explains that he keeps man enslaved and tortures him relentlessly. However, man submits willingly and even desires the *atroces délices* ("atrocious delights") Amor offers.

As we can see, this view of love is a restatement of the one presented in *Améthystes*. What is new in *Les Exilés* is Banville's more somber tone, the absence of any attempt to soften the seriousness of his ideas under any superficial lightness. What is new also is that he consistently approaches the subject through the mythological figure Amor or through some other symbolical incarnation, with the result that love's primordial and often monstrous nature stands out. In several poems love is represented by an echidna-like creature, both attractive and repulsive. "L'Antre" opens another dimension in linking love with the fallen angel. In a sinister and frightful cavern Hercules finds an aged monster seated on a pile of human bones. His eyes are bloodshot from weeping. Hercules promises to free him if he will come out, but the creature replies, "Non, je suis l'Amour" (No, I am Love). Over the entrance Hercules notices the words "Ici gémit l'éternel condamné" (Here moans the eternally condemned one), and the creature refers to himself as "le grand vaincu" (the great defeated one). Amor, who makes all human beings suffer, is himself an exile and, like the fallen angel, eternally condemned.

How can man be freed from his suffering and his exile? One of Banville's answers is through death. Some of the most exquisitely tender poems in Les Exilés are those that evoke the death of loved ones, such poems as "Pantin de la petite Jeanne," "Chio," "Le cher Fantôme," "Celle qui chantait," "Amédine Luther," and "L'Enamourée." Death is not seen as ugly or cruel; rather, it confers a new beauty and inspires infinite gentleness toward those to whom it comes. While Banville does not postulate the concept of eternal reward or final judgment, he clearly affirms a belief in immortality and resurrection. The most amply developed expression of his view of resurrection is "Le cher Fantôme." The poet does not grieve for his beloved, who has died, because her soul has taken flight toward the ethereal sky and plunges delightedly into the stream of joy and new life. But he weeps for her adorable form, her beautiful body. Then follows a meditation on the fate of the human body, its decay, its decomposition, the roots of trees penetrating into it and other plants being nourished by it, finally leaving no trace at all of the body. Troubled by this view, he has a dream in which he sees her in all her beauty and hears her voice, which assures him that her body lives rejuvenated by an apotheosis. The soul and the body, she says, are both irrevocably immortal. The new body resembles the old one but is made of a "more ethereal substance." Life is quickened, the spirit is made of light, and the senses, more perfect now, are able to see at once causes and effects.

There is hope even before death, hope that springs from the efforts of those who, knowing full well that they are doomed to exile on this earth, nonetheless hear in their souls the celestial harmonies of divine beginnings and strive to keep alive those echoes and to restore the original bliss of the universe. These are poets and heroes, who rise above common humanity, who see the suffering of the universe, and whose compassion extends to all beings. The pages of Les Exilés are filled with names of poets and other heroes. Such figures as Orpheus, Hercules, Aphrodite, Theseus, Roland, and Joan of Arc come to mind, individuals who have tried to civilize man, to reduce his suffering, to inspire him, and to uplift him. We encounter such names of poets as Homer, Eschylus, Dante, Shakespeare, Milton, Musset, and Heine, while individual poems pay tribute to Hesiod, Brizeux, Marceline Desbordes-Valmore, Rouvière, Gautier, Baudelaire, and George Sand. Banville stresses the idea that the poets of his time, suffering in their exile, have not forgotten the suffering of mankind. Nor have they compromised their dream of purity and beauty. Not only does Banville succeed in identifying the essential nature of each of these poets, and that in a sincere and unexaggerated manner, but in each poem his own style and verse form resemble those of the poet about whom he is writing.

The poet is an exile in the same way that all other beings are exiles, but he is able to lighten the exile of others. In addition, he is an exile in a narrower sense as well in his own society, since he more than other men retains in his soul the vision of paradise lost and becomes through his singularity a victim of other men. The attitude of his own society toward him is best illustrated by "Les Torts du cygne," a kind of fable. A solitary white swan on a silvery lake is insulted by black crows, who jeer at him because he is different. To them white is ugly. Why could he not be dressed in black?

> Un fait des plus élémentaires,
> C'est que le noir est distingué.
> C'est propre, c'est joli, c'est gai;
> C'est l'uniforme des notaires.
>
> (v. 7, p. 111)

> (One of the most elementary facts is that black is distinguished. It is clean, it is pretty, it is gay; it is the uniform of notaries.)

In this reference to bourgeois conformity there is a hint of Banville's funambulist manner. The swan is of course doomed to die but while the lark, the rose, and the nightingale mourn, the donkeys see no beauty in his song. While this fable may represent the poet's position in society in all ages, it is likely that Banville thought there were more donkeys in his own time. Yet the poet is not bitter. His love goes out even to those who misunderstand him. Though he bears affliction and scorn, he leaves behind him "patches of light" and his name will not perish ("Rouvière").

Banville tirelessly proclaims the gospel of the divinity of poetry and music. We have already seen how keenly he felt his own election to the privileged status of poet, privileged because poetry is the divine language of the universe. "Rhythm is everything," says Erinna, the leader of the young poetesses in "Erinna." "It elevates worlds and bears them singing into the ethereal plains." It is the mysterious law, both firm and flexible, partaking of the nature of "the holy laws of music" which maintain the harmony of the universe. In "A Georges Rochegrosse" Banville urges his stepson to learn "the language of the homeland," for heaven is not lost for those who in spite of all suffering and ills "still stammer the words whose origin is divine."

The prototype of the poet is Orpheus, the dominant figure in "La Cithare," which is also a little epic of the rise and fall of the gods. Orpheus is presented as the inventor of poetry and music, symbolized by the _cithare_ ("cither"). As he sings, all of nature responds as if animate. All beings are filled with love and fraternal feelings for each other. He then calls on all the Olympian gods in turn by name to listen to his song, in which can be heard "the storm of human sobs and from which gushes forth the life of the universe like an unrestrained river." He sees that gods and man are not part of the harmony of the celestial music, and the message of his song is an exhortation to rise toward the Light. He envisages a state in which death and night will cease. Centuries pass, and with them many gods and Orpheus also. The world is in exile and man feels abandoned:

L'homme désespéré ne voit devant ses yeux
Qu'un voile noir cloué sur la porte des cieux,
Et muré tout vivant dans la nuit ténébreuse,
Ne sait plus rien, sinon que sa douleur affreuse
Doit à jamais rester muette, et qu'il est seul.
(v. 7, p. 71)

(Man in despair sees before his eyes only a black veil nailed over the gates of heaven, and entombed alive in the dark night no longer knows anything except that his frightful suffering must forever remain unheard and that he is alone.)

The narrator-poet, however, closes the poem on a more hopeful note, stating that he still hears the soul of the cither exhaling its original cries toward heaven. At least the vision of what is divine has not been extinguished.

This brings us to the last poem of the collection, "Le Festin des Dieux," an evocation of paradise regained. Banville closes the circle. Centuries have passed since the exile of the gods. In a vision the poet sees a new palace on Mount Olympus. The gods are celebrating their return from exile. The image of a restored universe filled with beauty, joy, love, and harmony recalls the biblical vision of a new earth and a new heaven. Once again it is Aphrodite who speaks, fittingly so, for love is the message of the poets and the spirit of harmonious existence. She relates the events of the exile of the gods followed by their redemption by the poets: "...voici qu'en des âges plus doux / Les poètes nouveaux ont eu pitié de nous!" (v. 7, p. 209) (now in more gentle times new poets have had pity on us). She blesses mankind, even though it is through man's iniquity that the gods have suffered, and she closes her speech with her perception of the new world in which gods, man, and nature "are like an immense adoring family," and in which man is restored to his original glory. After the speech there is a scene of feasting: the rejuvenated gods, "thanks to the efforts of the poets," have overcome the horrors of death; Amor proposes a toast to the everlasting happiness of man; and the narrator hears "the marvelous song of the stars." This drama of fall and salvation has noticeable parallels with the Christian version. Like Christ, the Olympian gods descend to the human state.

It was not enough, says Aphrodite, that they already had human forms and emotions; they had to become mortal. However, unlike Christ's death, it is not their death that produces the salvation of man, at least not directly. It is the poets who assume Christ's role and save man and gods.

Les Exilés can be regarded as a refutation of the view that Banville's poetry is totally lacking in ideas. The collection expresses in a direct and serious manner without being obscured by facetiousness or obtrusive technical virtuosity the values he prizes. His admiration of Greek antiquity, his concern that the materialistic society of his time no longer has any feeling for the divine--these link him with other nineteenth-century writers and thinkers. His faith in man's immortality perhaps does not make him a typical nineteenth-century French writer. His preoccupation with the role of poetry and his faith in the poet's redemptive mission are an obsession with him. Numerous passages betray his desire to exalt the gods by making himself their ally against those who have dethroned them. Les Exilés more than his other collections has a flavor of antiquity in spite of the fact that it contains a uniquely Banvillean mixture of ancient and modern figures as well as ancient and modern styles. The long periods, the harangues, and the Homeric similes help to create an atmosphere suggestive of Greek antiquity, while at times enumerations, grandiose expressions, and verbal obsessions remind us of Hugo. Beauty of language and loftiness of thought and feeling confer a noble dignity on Les Exilés, making the collection a monument to the worth of man and underlining Banville's ultimate confidence in humanity.

Les Princesses

In 1874 Banville published a small collection of verse entitle Les Princesses composed of twenty-one sonnets, headed by the title poem "Les Princesses" and devoted to outstanding historical and mythological female figures, the majority of whom are drawn from antiquity: Semiramis, Pasiphaë, Omphale, Ariadne, Medea, Thalestris, Antiope, Andromeda, Helen, the Queen of Sheba, Cleopatra, Herodias, Messalina, Margaret of Scotland, Maria Stuart, Marguerite of Navarre, Lucretia Borgia, the Princesse de Lamballe, Madame Tallier, and the Princesse Borghèse. Banville had begun writing these sonnets in 1854 and included ten of the oldest in the first edition of Les Exilés. His short foreword of 1874 announces his intention "to evoke in twenty sonnets the images of those princesses with red lips and mysterious eyes who, having preserved the privilege of being adored as goddesses while the centuries have dispersed the last remains of the dust which was that of their proud bodies, have been the desire and the delight of the human race throughout the ages" (8). He hopes to suggest to his readers "ideas of triumph, pride, love, joy, power, bloodshed, and golden robes strewn with gems." The image of the princesses is always linked with "the splendor of scarlet" and "the fire of garnets." This is the color not only of hard, cold gems but also of blood and passionate lips.

What attraction did this subject have for Banville? Was it a hidden taste for violence, exotic color, and burning passion comparable to that of Flaubert in Salammbô, to that of Leconte de Lisle, or even to that of Heredia, who also wrote sonnets on Medea, Andromeda, and Cleopatra? Perhaps. But most of all, I think, these princesses are incarnations of strength, energy, and intensity of life, qualities that Banville sees lacking in his own age. They are a refreshing antidote to "Monsieur Scribe's vaudeville girls who, with smiles like those in romances, run after butterflies in their muslin dresses rendered more pretty by their invincible silk aprons with pink shoulder straps" (p. 216). With their vices and imperfections the princesses do not represent Banville's ideal of womanhood but they are a response to his nostalgia for a more basic heroic age. In their greatness they are for the most part also victims of their own animal passions. Unlike the heroes of antiquity in Les Exilés, they are not civilizers of mankind, but as in Améthystes the delights of love which their charms seem to promise usually lead to the suffering of their victims. They themselves are everywhere triumphant but appear superbly unaware of their own slavery to passion.

Like Améthystes, this collection is built on antithesis: most of the princesses are unusually beautiful but cruel; their charms are irresistible for men but their cruelty causes men to suffer. The contrast between their beauty and the cruelty and violence of many of them is harsh. Only two or three of them can be excepted. In general, the sonnets follow a uniform pattern, evoking the beauty and sensual charm of the princesses through a rather sumptuous imagery of gems and flowers, and suggesting in some way their violence. The opening sonnet characterizes the whole collection by promising the reader a rich and fabulous setting, murders, love, ingenuous lips, clothing revealing naked legs, blood, clasps of gold, rubies adorning the arms of the princesses, resplendent hair, snowy-white breasts, and lips like bloody flowers.

The combination of opposites as illustrated by fleurs sanglantes ("bloody flowers"), suggesting not only beauty and delicacy but also blood and cruelty, is perhaps Banville's most notable stylistic feature in Les Princesses. Cleopatra, as another example, is presented as "délices et boureau / Du monde" (delight and executioner of the world). The jewels which adorn the princesses suggest something hard and cold but the red of garnets and rubies also makes us think of blood and fire. Banville often takes advantage of the sonnet form by presenting one element in the octave and its opposite in the sestet. For example, in "Hérodiade" the octave emphasizes the apparent innocence, artlessness, and beauty of Herodias. The sestet suggests her sensuality and refers to the rich reflections of her gems. All of this prepares the shock effect of the last sentence: "...dans un plat d'or / Elle porte le chef sanglant de Jean-Baptiste" (v. 7, p. 242) (in a golden platter she carries the bloody head of John the Baptist). In a number of sonnets the second part of the contrast is contained in the last verse through the technique of suggestion, opening up a broad horizon of possibilities, a technique which Banville's younger contemporary Heredia was to perfect in his own sonnets.

Rimes Dorées

Rimes Dorées, published in 1869, the same year as the Occidentales, was written for the most part between 1863 and 1868. As Banville explains in his introductory remarks dated 1875, the ideas for most of these poems had been in his mind before the Occidentales (9). In sharp contrast to the inflexible unity of a collection such as Les Princesses, Rimes Dorées is perhaps the most heterogeneous and miscellaneous of his collections in mood, form, and even in subject matter. "These rhymes," he says, "were gilded in fact by those rays of the setting sun which sometimes have the joyous splendor of a sunrise" (p. 151). Banville's image is appropriate: it suggests an end, but also a beginning; the melancholy of evening, but also the hope of a new dawn. His own youth was far behind, but its memories were still fresh. The turmoil of 1848 in France and the early years of the Second Empire were also in the past, and the disaster of the Franco-Prussian War was in the unknown future. In a sense _Rimes Dorées_ could be considered a reflection of a static period for Banville, or, to use his own image, a gathering together of some of the sun's rays of the day gone by while waiting for a new dawn.

This collection has neither the grave dignity of _Les Exilés_ nor the facetious buffoonery of the _Odes Funambulesques_, but it contains poems written in the spirit of both. On the whole, the element of buffoonery is the lesser, and the excessive concern with technical virtuosity so characteristic of Banville's funambulist vein is not in evidence in _Rimes Dorées_. Its social criticism, though not a major component of the collection, concentrates on the lack of appreciation of beauty. Instead, his age is "courbé sur des écus" (stooped over its money), "L'Aube romantique" tells us.

For the most part _Rimes Dorées_ is positive in the sense that it celebrates what the poet cherishes most. Such poems as "Au Pays Latin" and "A la Jeunesse" express some of these values: love, beauty, the arts, liberty, dreams of heaven, glory, gay laughter, honor, and justice. The celebration of artists, fellow exiles, constitutes an important part of _Rimes Dorées_, although their state of exile is not stressed. "Au Pays Latin" names Hugo, Leconte de Lisle, Barbier, and Musset as members of the Latin Quarter's "divine race." "L'Aube romantique" recognizes the contributions of the Romantics, including the rehabilitation of Shakespeare, Ronsard, and others. It identifies the year 1830 as an age when beauty in its many artistic manifestations (poetry, drama, architecture, sculpture, and music) flourished, and it pays tribute to such writers, artists, and composers as Hugo, Gautier, Dorval, Berlioz, Sainte-Beuve, Barbier, Desbordes-Valmore, Sand, Balzac, Meyerbeer, Delacroix, and Gavarni. But all this is past, and the poet's thought takes an elegiac turn as he asks the nostalgic question, Ubi sunt:

> Où sont-ils, les poètes
> Qui nous faisaient des fêtes,
> Ces vaillants, ces grands coeurs,
> Tous ces vainqueurs...?
> (v. 3, p. 159)

(Where are they, the poets who prepared feasts for us, those valiant ones, those great-hearted ones, all those victors . . . ?)

Banville's greatest tribute is reserved for Ronsard in a longer poem at the end of the collection. His language and his praise are extravagant in apostrophizing Ronsard as a master of meter, sublime singer, divine bearer of the lyre, and new Pindar. Though Ronsard has been misunderstood, he has now become apotheosized and Banville evokes him in the rosy dawn, holding his lute in a fairy garden, honored by the other members of the Pléiade as well as by goddesses (including Venus herself), princesses, and the women he has made immortal in his poetry. As he takes up his lute and sings he is like another Orpheus. All things listen: even the stars suspend the music of their celestial concerts to hear him. He incarnates what for Banville is supreme: poetry and music. "La Rime est tout," he proclaims in "A Gabriel Marc." It is "le code et l'évangile / Et le degré qui monte aux paradis du ciel" (v. 3, p. 198) (Rhyme is everything. . . . the code and the gospel and the steps rising to the paradises of heaven).

Among the most striking poems in Rimes Dorées are six sonnets. The delicately restrained and elegiac "Maria Garcia" is one of them. Another is "Promenade galante." With its bittersweet mood and mixture of elegance, melancholy, charm, and silence, it recalls Verlaine's "Clair de lune," which predates it by a little more than a year. But perhaps the most original of them are the other four: "Le Musicien," "L'Echafaud," "La Blanchisseuse," and "Le Pompier." Written in the summer of 1868, they present little tableaux or scenes of life illustrating the mixture of misery and greatness of humanity, the heroism of simple people from lower stations of life, the lesser-known exiles. Each of these four sonnets provides a moment of illumination largely through the technique of presenting in the sestet some terse and unexpected contrast with what has preceded. "L'Echafaud" evokes the sordid world of crime and the cruelty of an execution, but the same dawn witnesses the birth of innocent children, "a reflection of heaven." An old man plays the violin evoking mankind's suffering and dreams, but the porter chases him away ("Le Musicien"). An attractive young girl is approached by an old libertine in "La Blanchisseuse," but she walks away free and with a dignified bearing, carrying her laundry. The fireman in "Le Pompier" dies on duty. His existence has created no stir in the world, but the inscription on his bracelet suggests the authenticity of his love for his wife.

In Les Exilés and the collections of a similar spirit Banville drops the mask of the clown and communicates to us an extraordinary awareness of and thirst for all that is beautiful. He shows us that his poetry is not without substance after all. The love of beauty, the vision of paradise, the grasp of the human condition, and the broad sympathy for all suffering beings make up the foundation of these collections. This is the serious Banville, the Banville whose poetic universe, however sober, does not crumble in despair and somehow does not keep out for long the light of hope.

Chapter Five

Other Poetry

Beginning with his first volume in 1842 Banville published at least one collection of poetry every decade of his life, the last publication, Dans la Fournaise, appearing the year after his death. Of his five remaining collections two date from the 1870s and can be classified as poésie de circonstance: Idylles Prussiennes and Roses de Noël. The other three--Nous Tous, Sonnailles et Clochettes, and Dans la Fournaise--were written during the last years of his life.

Idylles Prussiennes

Idylles Prussiennes appeared as a collection in 1871 a few months after the end of the Franco-Prussian War. Most of the sixty-five poems in the volume had already been published in Le National between October 3, 1870, and January 13, 1871. In his dedication of the book to Ildefonse Rousset, editor of Le National, Banville expresses his gratitude to Rousset for having included these poems on a regular basis: "Thanks to you, my friend, . . . I have been able to do what would have been the dream of every poet; that is, to write and compose under the very pressure of the events, in a newspaper, and with the public as a collaborator, as an inspirer and as an echo, these little poems which are always sincere" (1). It should be remembered that Banville for much of his life was a journalist by profession. But he had remained relatively aloof from involvement in social and political issues of his day and could hardly be regarded as a poète engagé, his Odes Funambulesques and his Occidentales notwithstanding. However, the disastrous Franco-Prussian War, which stunned France, awakened patriotic feelings in him and offered him an opportunity to combine lyric poetry with journalism. He cites as his authority for this approach the poet Goethe, who urged poets to seek inspiration in the events of the day and who maintained that all poetry is poetry of circumstance since reality furnishes the occasion for it, the poet's task being to give to the specific subject a general and poetic character (2).

Banville reasons that if such was Goethe's view even for ordinary reality how much more must this doctrine be true for exceptional times such as the Franco-Prussian War. Banville perceived himself to be a spectator of an epic moment in history. History itself seemed almost a personification of forces intervening directly and visibly before his very eyes, offering, even through tragedy and suffering, welcome relief from the prosaic gray of his society and age. The destruction and suffering he witnessed intensified his love and compassion for his country and for humanity, as did the numerous manifestations of courage and fortitude that heightened his image of humanity. He thought of himself as being on stage reciting his commentaries "by turns ironic, irritated, and enthusiastic, and releasing toward their target [his] sharp and whistling arrows" (p. 5).

For Barbey d'Aurevilly the _Idylles Prussiennes_ represented a rare phenomenon. Whereas in general, poets, even the greatest ones, remain imprisoned in a "certain manner," Banville is an exception, according to this critic, who finds in the _Idylles_ not only Banville's most beautiful poems but also a surprising newness, a complete change of manner after thirty years of "strictly unified poetic life" (3). Gone are the Harlequins, Pierrots, and the "bagatelles" and "soap bubbles" of the _Odes Funambulesques_. His "joyful imagination," Banville's distinctive feature, has given way to a much more gloomy poetry which Barbey d'Aurevilly calls _noires pièces_ ("gloomy pieces"), _élégies désespérées_ ("elegies of despair"), and _poésie d'écrasés_ ("poetry of the downtrodden"). In the collection he finds despair stronger than hope and judges that "all the pieces in . . . _Idylles_ are superb" (4).

It is difficult to accept Barbey d'Aurevilly's assessment without modification. If on the whole the tone of this work is serious and if Banville's lyricism tends to be more elegiac than in most of his previous volumes, this is a matter of degree rather than a complete about-face. The collection is not totally lacking in puns, sarcasm, and other funambulistic techniques associated with the _Odes Funambulesques_ or the

Occidentales. Nor is its broad human compassion new; we find this abundantly in Les Exilés. But perhaps one of the features that sets it apart from earlier collections is a certain sense of immediacy arising from Banville's strong emotional involvement in the events inspiring these poems. In the Odes Funambulesques Banville set himself the task of creating comedy largely through techniques of versification. While references to people and events of his time are abundant they are pretexts only. The starting point is not so much feeling as technique. In the Idylles, on the other hand, he is more concerned with the intensity of his feelings than with technical experimentation. It is important to observe, for example, that all the poems of the collection are written in octosyllabic quatrains.

The most immediate of these feelings, given the circumstances, are love of his country and hatred of the invading enemy. The target of the arrows to which Banville refers in his preface is the invader, the Prussians rather than the Germans, the Prussian leaders rather than the Prussian people, and even more specifically Bismarck more than Emperor Wilhelm and Field Marshal von Moltke. There is perhaps some irony in the fact that Goethe, whose philosophy Banville invokes for the Idylles, and Heine, whom he admired so much, belonged to the very nation the collection presumably attacks. But the greatness of these and other German artists is not diminished in his eyes by what Prussian leaders are doing. In fact, he feels solidarity with them and sees them as a reproach to "Monsieur de Bismarck" and his emperor ("La Flèche"). It is true that on rare occasions, such as in "Aux Compagnies de guerre du dix-huitième bataillon," he denounces the invaders in violent terms such as envahisseur exécré ("execrated invader"), ces maudits ("those cursed ones"), le Vandale, and ce rustre ("this bumpkin"). Other poems of condemnation and denunciation include "Attila," "Le Cavalier," and "Les Enfants morts."

But, on the whole, Banville's attacks on Prussian leaders and the Prussian mentality as it is incarnated by them do not take the form of invective. His arms are those of the Odes Funambulesques and the Occidentales: caricature and buffoonery, effective weapons against the powerful. "Raillery, irony, simian mimicry," Banville states in an article dated November 1, 1880, in Le National, "is an art of the oppressed and the slave, the vengeance of the oppressed against the oppressor, of the weak against the strong" (5). Perhaps he also had in mind the example of Victor Hugo's Les Châtiments, in which the poet's contempt for Louis Napoleon found powerful expression through parody and sarcasm.

Ambition and thirst for power are the most frequent targets of Banville's attack, and Bismarck is the chief incarnation of hunger for power. In "La Lune" Banville imagines a conversation in which the Prussian minister tells Wilhelm of his plans to conquer all the other countries of the globe. Once this has been done and everyone has been made into a Prussian there will be nothing left to conquer, for the moon, he adds, cannot be taken. Moltke, however, replies, "Yes, I have made my calculations; it can be taken!" But even that is not enough. In "Scapin tout seul" a new "acteur bouffon" appears wearing the costume of the valet Scapin. Playing the role of the boastful soldier, he brags about his power and accomplishments: he has captured Mars and Jupiter and his sword can split mountains. The claims he makes for his power over nature are patently ridiculous and absurd: pigeons crossing the line of battle will be judged by the council of war; if the wind should betray him it will be tried; and if the stars give information to the enemy they will be shot. It is perhaps not necessary to explain, as Banville does at the end of the poem, that he is comparing Bismarck to this buffoon.

Emperor Wilhelm comes under fire also. "L'Empereur" represents him at the height of his power, feared by all and believing himself the equal of the gods. Suddenly there is an enormous burst of laughter. Who would dare laugh at him? It is the laughter of the real emperor coming from Charlemagne's tomb and making Germany tremble. "Un vieux Monarque" recalls "Scapin tout seul," but this time it is the Kaiser who is dressed as a clown. "A Meaux, en Brie" brings about the association with the spirit of buffoonery in still another way. Wilhelm, finding himself in the town of Meaux, encounters a troop of acrobats and clowns in the public square and comes face to face with their leader Bilboquet: "Ils se dévisagent, le prince / Des bouffons et le roi des rois" (v. 4, p. 109) (They stare at each other, the prince of clowns and the king of kings). It is as if one is the mirror image of the other. The clown sees the copper eagle on the helmet of the emperor. Here Banville amuses himself with punning and playing with the word aigle ("eagle"). In order to follow what he does it is necessary to recall that the great seventeenth-century writer and orator Bossuet, for a time bishop of Meaux, was known as the Aigle de Meaux. To return to the poem, we find that the narrator continues as follows:

> Alors, ôtant son feutre glabre,
> Que chaque ouragan boussuait,
> Et qui fut fait à coups de sabre,
> Il dit ces mots: O Bossuet!
> (v. 4, p. 109)

> (Then taking off his bare felt hat, which would bulge out in any storm and which was made with sabre strokes, he said these words: Oh Bossuet!)

The fact that everybody then dines on young eagle, which Banville suggests may not be bad fare, seems like a non sequitur. The end of the poem registers surprise that a bird of yellow copper has now become the eagle of Meaux.

The extent to which all this caricature of the enemy expresses hatred of him may be a debatable point. The other side of the coin, Banville's love of France, seems at any rate more convincing. The buffoonery is replaced by a more direct manner of expression, which for the most part has a ring of sincerity. Banville's personal attitude is perhaps best reflected in "A la Patrie," a poem of patriotic confession in which he declares that he has always loved his country, but now that it has been humiliated his love has changed to fierce adoration. The dominant characteristic of the image he presents of his country is heroism, from the leaders down to the common soldiers and the ordinary people. Ordinary soldiers are glorified in their eagerness to die for their country.. The people of France are presented as equally courageous and indomitable, both in the provinces and in Paris.

Paris especially exemplifies the virtues that Banville exalts. "Bonne Fille" presents what Banville imagines to be the Prussians' view of Paris--as a courtesan to be seduced and enjoyed. But he warns them that her embrace will be savage, she will tear them, and her mouth will spit fire and death upon them. Von Moltke is dismayed to learn from two hideous hags named Famine and Épouvante ("Terror") that neither one has been able to subjugate the city. Its inhabitants stand shoulder to shoulder, equal before death, and beneath the explosion of bombs red blood is mingled with blue ("Rouge et Bleu").

"Vingt-neuf Janvier" marks the moment of grief when defeat has become a reality. The tired troops, downcast and gloomy, return from battle. Banville calls it a heartbreaking sight and imagines that even the voice of the sea grieves for them. Yet hope is not lost. Like the dying lion insulted by the cowardly fox in "Le Lion," France can say, "Je meurs, mais je suis le Lion!" (v. 4, p. 177) (I am dying but I am still the lion!). There are other visions of hope. In "Espérance," for example, the intensely fervent invocation to the fatherland--bleeding, beloved, and seemingly dead--is followed by an expression of faith in the recovery of its strength. The tide of fortunes will change, for fluttering before it is "the blue veil of hope."

In some of Banville's intensely patriotic poems containing visions of his country's military accomplishments, promises of cannon and machine-gun fire, and flaming death to the enemy, he seems to have forgotten for the moment his uncompromising condemnation expressed in his _Odes Funambulesques_ and his _Occidentales_ of all manifestations of militarism in his country. But the _Idylles_ were written in the heat of emotion, as the events happened. Goethe's ideal, as Banville recalls it, was to confer on specific events a general and poetic character. The danger for the poet inspired by contemporary events is perhaps that he may not succeed in raising them from their particular reality to a general significance. The failure to rise above a narrowly partisan level is one of the weaknesses of the _Idylles_. But a large number of them fortunately achieve a wider vision. They show that the horrors of war know no political or national distinctions. To begin with, the title _Idylles Prussiennes_ is bitterly ironic: nothing could be less idyllic than the events these poems relate. When Bismarck in "Le Cavalier" declares, "Soyons des faiseurs de corps morts" (v. 4, p. 10) (Let us be makers of dead bodies), he is stating that the object of war is to kill, a principle governing all participants.

War as a phenomenon of human existence is incomprehensible to Banville and unreal, a horrible nightmare ("Cauchemar"). The Prussians invading French soil are like phantoms from the distant past repeating the ravages of the Germanic tribes during the time of the Roman Empire, and once they have disappeared no trace of their reality will be left. To the question, "Où sont donc ces spectres errants?" (Where are those wandering specters then?), the mountains and the plains will reply, "Nous n'en savons plus rien!" (v. 4, p. 37) (We do not know anything about it any more). From other perspectives war makes no sense either. The little girl in "La Fillette" goes to an open market to sell shell fragments. The sight of the sparrow in "Le Moineau" drinking rain water from a hollow bomb fragment leads the poet to reflect that perhaps war is good for something after all. Its hideous massacre, those pale bodies nailed to the ground, those broken heads, those pierced bellies, that charnel house with its pestilential smell make it possible in the end for the little bird to drink. The confrontation of the two totally unequal sides of this absurd argument with its bitter sarcasm reinforces the senselessness of war. But perhaps there is another dimension here: this little bird _du ciel_ ("from heaven") is not aware of the ugliness of war. The world goes on; war is only man's doing. Glory and power are illusory and ephemeral, and even kings become carrion ("Les deux Soleils").

Where Banville's perspective particularly goes beyond the superficial aspects of the events which inspire the _Idylles_ is in his broad view of human suffering and his compassion, which knows no distinction between victor and vanquished. Far from condemning the German people, he feels sorry for them as victims of the ruthless and unscrupulous rulers of Prussia. The young Bavarian soldier in "Le Bavarois" is the spokesman for all the non-Prussian Germans sent to the front lines by Bismarck, who reserves less dangerous roles for the Prussians. "Travail Stérile" takes the form of a dialogue in which businessmen, bankers, laborers, tradesmen, and other citizens from many parts of Germany all recognize that they are victims of the King of Prussia.

The poet's pity goes out to all the bereaved, whether German or French. Young German women, pale, worn, dressed in black, walk almost ghostlike, holding their little undernourished children in their skinny hands. The prospect of a greater Germany pales into insignificance in comparison with the more fundamental issue of life and death. Their husbands, the fathers of these children, are gone, their whereabouts unknown; they lie perhaps in the green grass of some forgotten field, their eyes sightless and their breasts gashed by wounds ("Les Allemandes"). A French father, speechless with grief at the realization that his sixteen-year-old son, hardly more than a rosy-cheeked boy on the threshold of life, is dead, can only say, "God save France!" ("Les Pères"). The mourning of the bereaved is not only for soldiers. War sometimes injects strange irony into an existence. An example is "Celle qui reste," a little human drama in which a girl and her mother are both hit by a shell. The mother in all her poverty and hardship had cheerfully made sacrifices for her daughter's future happiness, and dreamed of dying weary but happy in the knowledge that the daughter's welfare was assured. But now fate in an instant has changed the course of their lives, for the daughter is killed while the mother survives.

Banville's greatest tenderness is reserved for the dead. The poems in which he evokes them are among the most moving in all his poetry. This tenderness is extended to the enemy as well, for in death friend and foe are equal. He is especially touched by the fact that many of the victims of battle are the extremely young, sixteen or eighteen years old, cut down when their life has hardly begun:

> O mobiles, gais et superbes,
> Si voisins de l'enfance encor,
> Avec vos visages imberbes
> Et vos cheveux aux reflets d'or!
> ("Le Jour des Morts")
> (v. 4, p. 60)

(Oh militiamen, gay and proud, still so close to childhood, with your beardless faces and your hair reflecting gold!)

One of these, a Prussian boy in "Un Prussien mort," is lying in the cutting wind of an open field. A volume of Pindar is in his pocket. Would he have become a poet, this eighteen-year-old boy, "parti bien avant l'heure / Jeune et pur, sans avoir pleuré" (v. 4, p. 34) (departed well before his time, young and pure, without having wept)?

One of the most touching and delicate of these poems is "Le Jour des Morts." The speaker scatters flowers to the four winds, offering them along with his tears to the dead soldiers. The first few quatrains are filled with apostrophes ("O soldats! ô morts inconnus," etc.), but with the question, "Où dormez-vous?" (v. 4, p. 60) (Where are you sleeping?), the poet begins an elegiac meditation in a calmer mood. The mystery of death itself is deepened by the fact that the location of the dead is not known. But wherever they are, their ashes mingled with the earth will enrich the land. When peace comes, their sisters, mothers, and wives will search for the place where they are sleeping in a spring landscape made more beautiful by their death. Futile as these efforts may seem, these devoted women do not give up their dreams of finding their loved ones, and, looking toward the stream or the hill crowned with a trembling aspen, they say to each other, "C'est peut-être là!" (Perhaps it is there!).

When Banville published the Idylles Prussiennes in Le National he attached titles such as Feuilles Volantes, Bellum, Les Vandales, La Légende, Les Ames, and others to various parts of the collection. These recall the subtitles used by Hugo in Les Châtiments or in Les Contemplations. Perhaps Banville's subtitles indicate that he was attempting to create a work of more than ordinary dimensions, a satire with an epic scope. Whatever his reasons, all these subtitles were dropped after having been included in Le National. Possibly he realized that the dream of the elevated epic or the Hugolian satire was not in his temperament. The final irony of this collection already full of ironies is that, not only is it not successful satire, but that much of it is among Banville's best elegiac poetry.

Roses de Noël

One of the striking features of Banville's poetry is its protean changeability. He moves with ease from the cynical but witty conversational monologue of a Musset to Hugolian hyperbole; he passes effortlessly from the rhythms of Villon to those of Charles d'Orléans, Clément Marot, or Ronsard; he captures accents of André Chénier or of Baudelaire; and at other times his sculptured miniatures make us think of Gautier or Heredia. In Roses de Noël we find yet another dimension, the poetry of memories and the family. Here his unrivaled master is Lamartine but, although some of the poems in the collection compel us to recall the Lamartine of "Milly" and of "La Vigne et la Maison," they do not achieve the richness and fullness of orchestration of the bard of Mâcon. Instead, in their apparently artless and spontaneous simplicity, Banville often captures very nearly the accents of that touching Romantic songstress Marceline Desbordes-Valmore, who poured out her feelings with the candor of a child.

Banville appears to have had some misgivings about this collection. He was not accustomed to writing confessional poetry relating to his personal life and family, having published fewer than a dozen poems of this kind, scattered here and there in various collections. He appeared to doubt the validity of personal poetry as art. Composed between 1843 and 1878, the thirty poems making up Roses de Noël were written for his mother on the occasion of her birthday, February 16, and her saint's day, November 19. The collection bears the dedication "A ma mère, Madame Claude-Théodore de Banville, née Elisabeth-Zélie Huet." Apparently, however, Banville originally had no intention of publishing these poems. But in 1878, the year of his mother's death, they appeared with this explanation given in a foreword dated November 19, 1878: "But in giving them to the public today I am obeying the wish, emphatically expressed, of one who will never be absent from me and whose eyes see me. Moreover, upon reflection, I think she is right as always; for the poet who wants to suffer, to live with the people and share with them the highest hopes, keeps nothing hidden from them and must always be prepared to show his whole soul" (6). Yet the foreword opens with the following declaration: "The poems that follow are not works of art," continuing a little further on, "Almost never is one a good craftsman when one writes under the pressure of a real feeling at the very time when one experiences it" (p. 299).

At the rate of two poems a year between 1843 and

1878 Banville should have written some seventy poems. Possibly ill health and "agitations" in his life to which he refers in his foreword (p. 299) prevented him from writing that many, but it is tempting to speculate that perhaps he published only the best ones. In a sense also it is misleading to think of these "intimate" poems as expressions of feelings experienced twice a year on specific occasions. Rather, they reflect a lifelong relationship between the poet and his mother. Possibly, too, Banville's concern about their artistic quality conceals a deeper concern, especially in a Post-Romantic, Parnassian poetic climate: the fear of displaying intimate feeling.

Banville's purpose in Roses de Noël might be summed up partly by a passage in "Exil," in which he says that he is sending his mother his kiss, his tender caress, his soul, and his voice, as expressions of his love. But he also had his eye on le vert laurier ("the green laurel"), with which he was concerned all his life. Possibly with the example of Ronsard in the back of his mind, he had the conscious ambition of immortalizing his mother (and perhaps himself):

Ainsi je prie ayant, comme un bon ouvrier,
Le désir de gagner quelque brin de laurier
Pour parer de renom ta vieillesse adorée;
Je voudrais, conquérant l'immortelle durée,
Que fleurissant toujours malgré les noirs hivers,
Ta mémoire pût vivre à jamais dans mes vers.
("Comme un jour")
(v. 5, p. 336)

(Thus I pray, having like a good workman the desire to earn some sprig of laurel to embellish your adored old age with renown; I would wish that, overcoming immortal time, your memory, flowering always in spite of dark winters might be able to live forever in my verses.)

It is clear that Madame Banville's role in her son's life was of immense importance. She was many things to him. "Toute mon âme" recalls how she loved him and nursed him. She was an inspiration not only to him but also to his sister, instilling in them love of beauty and disdain for vulgarity. Banville acknowledges his debt to her for having opened the world of poetry for him ("Ta Voix," "Le Ruisseau"). He remembers her especially as a comforter and recalls scenes from childhood when he and his sister would run to their mother's lap to receive her kisses, which would banish all their pain.

She is something more to the man-poet. She assumes symbolic dimensions, becoming part of the stream of eternal time in which she lives on through her son. "Et c'est toi que tu sens en moi lutter, poursuivre / Le but..." (It is you whom you feel struggling in me, pursuing the goal), he says in "Le Ruisseau," the opening poem, adding this unusual image: "Telle, aux humides prés, la Naïade ravie, / Dont le sort incertain est celui du ruisseau, / Rêveuse, en flots d'argent voit s'écouler sa vie" (v. 5, p. 302) (Thus, in watered meadows, the delighted Naiad whose fate is that of the stream, dreamy, sees her life flowing away in a silvery stream). This mythological element may seem out of place in such personal poetry, but the concept of a mythological figure partaking of the essence of nature and at the same time being distinct from it embodies exactly the relationship Banville wishes to express; namely, that in her son's life she sees her own, at the same time standing back from it and viewing it as in a mirror.

Earlier I referred to a history of marital happiness in the Banville family. The handful of poems scattered here and there in other collections and devoted to Banville's sister, wife, stepson, mother, father, and his native village all reflect the happiness and affection he knew in the family where he grew up and in the one he founded himself. Roses de Noël is the most complete poetic document relating to the former, and although all its poems are addressed to his mother they have biographical value to the extent that they show Banville's perception of his family and of his own life. "Extase" celebrates the beginning, the birth of his mother, an example of the mystery of human beginnings, a soul leaving heaven in order to know terrestrial suffering and struggles. For her parents the event brings indescribable joy. In that "moment ineffable" they cry and smile and, swelling with pride, they cover their little Zélie with kisses. The love with which she is received as she comes into the world, she passes on amply to her own children. The portrait of his mother that Banville allows us to put together from his Roses is no doubt idealized. She possessed a special kind of beauty both physical and spiritual, a kind of noble serenity and a naturally happy and affectionate temperament. Her gentle voice was his "poetry" and "his first feast" ("Douces Larmes"). Her smile was like the sun bringing warmth into a wintry day, and her eyes were like the water reflecting the sky ("Ton Sourire"). What continues to impress the poet is that she retained her youthfulness. "Les ans ne te vieillissent pas" (v. 5, p. 323) (The years do not age you), he exclaims in "Feuilles mortes."

Other poems recall Moulins and the family home. It was in Moulins, in "le grand jardin de fleurs" (the large garden of flowers), that his grandparents looked after the little girl who was to become his mother ("Les Jardins"). Time passes and Banville evokes "the joyful house" and sees his mother "in front of the rose-clad wall" or among the trees, everywhere spreading her infinite grace ("Les Oiseaux"). In "Fleurs d'hiver" some winter flowers that will not even open have the power to evoke "les jardins que nous avons connus" (the gardens we have known), a felicitous image, which with its plural "jardins" expands the vision to a more general past including Moulins:

> O notre cher Moulins! Devant nos yeux éclate
> Parmi nos souvenirs gracieux et pensifs
> Un éblouissement de rose et d'écarlate;
> Et les deux pièces d'eau, la verdure, les ifs,
> Nous voyons tout, les Dieux de pierre, la
>   rocaille,...
>
> (v. 5, p. 310)

> (Oh our dear Moulins! Before our eyes a dazzling brightness of rose and scarlet bursts forth among our gracious and pensive memories; and the two bodies of water, the greenery, the yew trees, we see everything, the stone gods, the stonework.)

As in Lamartine's "Milly," but on a miniature scale, memory returns to visit all the corners of the native village.

"Zélie enfant" presents a portrait of Banville's sister, carefree, radiant in the dawn, running in the grass, hair flying in the wind, happy and grave at the same time, her eyes innocent and her mouth like a little rose. But by far the most complete evocation of his childhood is to be found in "Pourquoi seuls?" As memory is piled upon memory the poet's emotion is heightened and he feels an urgency to lose himself in this sea of the past. He invites his mother to share these memories, which have the power to illuminate the darkness of life, an idea to which he returns several times in the collection.

After the happy childhood comes separation:

> Entre nous, ô tourment!
> Sont les villes sans nombre et leur
> bourdonnement,
> Le temps, les nuits, les jours, le silence,
> l'espace,
> Les collines, les bois, les cieux, le vent
> qui passe.
>
> ("Les Oiseaux")
> (v. 5, p. 321)

(Between us, oh torment, are cities without number and their buzzing, time, nights, days, silence, space, hills, woods, skies, the passing wind.)

He has drunk disgust and bitterness and learned that other kisses betray ("Douces Larmes"). He has found that in his "arid days" all is vanity and lies, that nothing lasts, and that hope and dreams are like roses whose petals are carried off by the night wind. Only his mother's love has remained as a talisman for him ("Feuilles mortes"). The next step is death.

His father had died in 1846, but it was Zélie's death in 1867 that left the deepest impression on the rest of the poems in Roses de Noël. Most of them from this time onward console his mother and affirm his faith in God. "Dieu nous rend tout ce qu'il nous enlève" (v. 5, p. 328) (God gives us back everything he takes from us), he proclaims in "Pour nous deux." He imagines Zélie instructing him to take their mother in his arms and kiss her for them both. Banville feels the presence of the departed. From their "séjour divin" (heavenly home) they are watching those who remain behind weeping. He assures his mother in "Leurs Lèvres" that his father and sister want to console them, that their spirit is in the air, and their voice is in the gentle sighing of the fragrant flowers.

The dead whom they love have already been awakened to a new life ("Vers le ciel").

Just three years before his mother's death he wrote "Nous voilà tous," his finest evocation of resurrection. This poem closes the circle with his vision of the family reunited. But it is more than that; it is a kind of apocalypse in which he sees every moment and hears every voice in the awakening:

> L'air est plein du frisson des ailes des
>   oiseaux
> Et des âmes des morts et du souffle des
>   Anges;
> Celui vers qui toujours monte un flot de
>   louanges
> Et qui de nos douleurs a fait des voluptés,
> Nous dit alors tout bas: Voici l'heure.
>   Écoutez.
> Et plus faibles qu'un vol d'abeilles sur
>   les mousses,
> Nous entendons les voix qui nous semblaient
>   si douces
> Jadis; car rien ne meurt, la tombe n'a
>   rien pris
> De la clarté sereine et pure des esprits,
> Et Dieu, qui les créa dans leur splendeur
>   première,
> N'a pas fait du néant avec de la lumière.
>   (v. 5, pp. 345-46)

(The air is filled with the shudder of birds' wings and of the souls of the dead and of the breath of the angels; He toward whom always rises a stream of praise and who out of our pain has made pleasure then says to us quietly: The time has come. Listen. And more gentle than a flight of bees on the moss we hear the voices that seemed so sweet to us long ago; for nothing dies, the tomb has taken none of the serene and pure clarity of the souls, and God who created them has not produced oblivion out of light.)

The last poem, "A Celle qui me voit," written after Madame Banville's death, imagines her "in the ethereal spaces filled with wings." Although she cannot read this poem they are united by prayer. Their cherished memories have strengthened his faith, and he reaffirms his confidence that Christ's blood has been shed for all and that, when earthly suffering ceases, he will be reunited with her, receiving her maternal kiss on his forehead as he did when he was a child.

It seems natural to refer to Banville as the poet of the _Odes Funambulesques_ or even of _Les Exilés_, but who would think of calling him the poet of _Roses de Noël_? And yet this collection deserves a better fate. The fact that the poems in it are unpretentious and sometimes have about them an air of improvisation makes their art seem unobtrusive, but we should be skeptical of Banville's statement that they are not art. Few poets have held their vocation in higher esteem than Banville, and it is difficult to imagine him writing any verse without art. But in its personal lyricism the collection is unique in Banville's work. In its celebration of memory and the past it is the most Romantic of his collections and deserves more recognition than it has had as poetry of the family. It is not easy to think of another poet who, in the intensity of his joy in living, clings more avidly to every moment, unwilling to let any pass into oblivion, for the past contains the dawn of tomorrow:

> Ah! gardons bien, gardons comme de saintes
>   proies
> Tout ce qui fut à nous, les douleurs et les
>   joies,
> Les mots qui nous charmaient, les cris
>   mélodieux,
> Les chagrins étouffants, les retours, les
>   adieux,
> Les gais soleils brillant dans la campagne
>   verte,
> Le souvenir saignant comme une plaie
>   ouverte,
> Et l'aile de la brise et le parfum des
>   bois,
> Les chants, les pas, les jeux, les sourires,
>   les voix,
> Et quand l'ombre nous gagne, emplissons-nous
>   d'aurore.
>
> ("Nos Proies")
> (v. 5, p. 347)

(Ah! let us keep like sacred prey all that was ours, the griefs and the joys, the words that charmed us, the melodious cries, the stifling sorrows, the returns, the farewells, the cheerful sunlight on the green countryside, the memories bleeding like an open wound, and the wings of the breeze and the fragrance of the forest, the songs, the steps, the games, the smiles, the voices, the songs, and when the shadows overcome us, let us fill ourselves with the dawn.)

Later Poetry

After the death of his mother in 1878 Banville devoted himself largely to prose and to the writing of plays. In 1880 he joined the staff of Le Gil Blas as a columnist. Here he found time to publish some poetry on a regular basis mostly between December, 1883, and March, 1884. Later in 1884 these poems were collected and published under the title Nous Tous. That year illness came back again to haunt him. Nevertheless, he was able to remain active and productive. In 1888 he left Le Gil Blas to write for L'Écho de Paris, to which he contributed poetry every week or two. The poems that appeared here between May 19, 1888, and May 27, 1890, were to form the collection Sonnailles et Clochettes published in 1890. During the last decade of his life and especially since his illness in 1884 Banville was spending more and more time in seclusion in his country home at Lucenay near his beloved Moulins. Here, when he was not writing, he would walk in the familiar places of his childhood and enjoy the warmth and affection of his wife and stepson Georges, who contributed frontispieces to his books and did occasional research for him. In the night between the twelfth and the thirteenth of March, 1891, on the eve of his sixty-eighth birthday he died. According to his wishes no funeral oration took place (7). But the voice of his lyre was not silent yet; the following year Charpentier, under the title Dans la Fournaise published a posthumous collection of poems which Banville had written between 1876 and his death and some of which had previously appeared in L'Echo de Paris and Le Gil Blas.

Except for some two dozen poems in Dans la Fournaise all the poetry of Banville's last three collections began as newspaper copy contributed on a regular basis to meet deadlines. Until the end he was obliged to write for a living. Perhaps these circumstances guaranteed quantity more than quality. Nous Tous with ninety-six poems, Sonnailles et Clochettes with sixty-two, and Dans la Fournaise with seventy-seven, are among the largest of his collections but unfortunately not among his best. In them he was trying to realize his dream of "marrying poetry with the newspaper." He celebrates what he calls "le journalisme poétique," stating his conviction that there is a place in the newspaper for "that poetry of a very French vein, lively, ironic, precise, and lyrical," a legacy of Villon (8). His aim was to reach a large number of readers. "Isn't it attractive to rhyme from day to day for the readers of the newspaper; that is to say, for every one?" he asks in the foreword of Sonnailles et Clochettes. He calls these poems caprices légers ("light caprices") or "petits poèmes." In a sense he was doing what he had done in the Idylles Prussiennes, except that his subject was not history but everyday life. Indeed, nowhere else in his poetry is the element of realism, understood as a reflection of everyday prosaic life with emphasis on its uglier aspects, as pronounced as in these last three collections.

While it cannot be contested that Banville perceived daily life with unusual intensity, his taste can occasionally be regarded as questionable (9). He treats the most banal subjects: the weather, styles, smoking, restaurant food, hats, umbrellas, and ladies' garments. These are all part of the reality of modern life as he observes it in Paris. His love of Paris is evident. The city provides a veritable comédie humaine; in fact, it is an invention of the late Balzac, he tells us in "Sursum" (Sonnailles et Clochetes). Paris represents "la Vie / Moderne, frémissante, avide, inassouvie, / Belle de douleur calme et de sévérité" (modern life, pulsating, eager, unsated, beautiful in its calm sorrow and severity); and its sights, activities, and occupations are endlessly rich ("Aimer Paris," Dans la Fournaise).

There is a seamy side to its life as well. Violence, crime, passions, prostitution, and the cult of matter are part of it. It is a kind of jungle, "Toute entière livrée à la matière vile / Et d'où le chaste azur s'efface et disparaît" (entirely given up to vile matter and where the chaste azure is erased and disappears), and men are like panting, ferocious beasts ("La Forêt," Dans la Fournaise). "La Nuit" (Sonnailles et Clochettes) is the best of several poems evoking the night life of the city. Also comparing Paris to a dark forest inhabited by wild animals, it conveys the spirit of the city's night life through the image of the prostitute: the Seine in its bed sobs and stretches like a courtesan, while the poet kisses the burning fire on the two lips of Rhyme. Meanwhile, publishers count their money, prostitutes practice their profession, and criminals are out on the street. But Banville can never long remain earthbound; fantasy is as real as matter, and the miraculous is normal rather than exceptional. At the end of the poem we find a larger vision reminding us that life is not only the degradation of the streets:

> Et dans l'immensité des cieux
> On voit au-dessus de nos fanges
> Comme un long choeur silencieux
> Errer les figures des Anges.

(And in the immensity of the skies can be seen roaming above our mire, like a long and silent choir, the figures of Angels.)

It is worth noting what a modern and even prophetic ring Banville's perceptions of everyday reality have. The life he presents is so often close to the problems of the twentieth century. Crime, prostitution, and poverty are of course not only modern social problems, but his ability to place them in the context of a large city makes them appear modern. The criminal he presents, for example, is the teen-age hoodlum, the mugger, so familiar to inhabitants of large cities. As for the prostitute, he sees her with a certain sympathy as a victim. "Nous sommes des êtres fictifs / Créés par vos désirs lubriques" (We are fictitious beings created by your lubricious desires), the prostitutes exclaim in "Les Tristes" (Nous Tous). In a deeply touching poem, "Petit Noël" (Nous Tous), Banville presents the pathos of poverty through a small boy, thin, sickly and in tatters, who on the night of Christmas prays that Jesus will let him have a new pair of shoes as a gift and perhaps, he adds, a few candies in them.

The World Fair of 1889 provided Banville with the opportunity to acknowledge scientific and technological progress. "Tour Eiffel" (Sonnailles et Clochettes) is a serious ode to the famous tower, a structure erected for the fair. More accurately, the poem celebrates the progress of science and ends with a vision of science as a liberating force that will improve human life by reducing suffering. But even in his rare incursions into the domain of science, it is usually the poetic imagination that triumphs. In "Concurrence" (Sonnailles et Clochettes), for example, the fireworks and the latest inventions displayed at the fair become images in terms of which a heavenly display, a kind of celestial World Fair perhaps, is evoked. The storm is the fireworks, and the cherubim open the fair, which is attended by such notable figures as Saturn, Venus, and Sirius. In the thunder and the flashes of lightning God, the supreme scientist and poet, "puissamment lyrique / Lutte avec Edison / A sa façon" (powerfully lyrical, is competing with Edison in his own way); and the "ingénieur des mondes / Construit dans le plein ciel / Sa Tour Eiffel" (the engineer of worlds is building his Eiffel Tower in the open sky).

In some instances Banville's perception of social problems might even apply to our own time. In "Carnaval" (Sonnailles et Clochettes) a man is asked why he is not dressed in a carnival costume. His reply might well remind us of the way some contemplative cults of our day are sometimes viewed: he says he is disguised as a young man analyzing himself and looking at his navel. In another poem, "Les Grâces" (Dans la Fournaise), Banville identifies three great social ills by stating that the three Graces of Greek mythology have been replaced in modern times by "Absinthe, Névrose et Morphine." Our age might call them alcoholism, mental illness, and drug abuse. Great concern is felt nowadays in much of the world about a shortage of energy resources. But we are not the first to know such fears. The speaker in a poem dated December 23, 1890, laments that soon the earth's resources will be exhausted. Wild animals will be extinct, vegetable life will disappear, the fire of the bowels of the earth will be replaced by snow, coal and other minerals will be exhausted, and hunger and disease will prevail ("Fleur," Dans la Fournaise).

Contemporary issues often lead back to what is more permanent in the human condition. Even as the speaker reflects on the depletion of the earth's resources, a lovely girl passes by and he is reminded that, while the earth may well be old, "Comme la jeune fille est jeune!" (How young the young girl is!). Love and beauty are not exhaustible like mineral resources. But the other side of the coin, equally a part of the human condition, is the corruption of the flesh, a state powerfully suggested in an image in "Triomphe" (Dans la Fournaise): an attractive and seductive woman is presented, for whom the men will die or go mad. But when the wind lifts her dress one can see a wound festering, with edges yellow and green, infested with crawling worms, a sight that can hardly be contemplated without a shudder of disgust and revulsion.

Apart from their emphasis on the more prosaic aspects of reality, these last three collections offer little that is new, and as poetry they are not among Banville's best. Their sheer volume contributes to their repetitiveness and eventually their monotony. But when placed in the context of his total poetic output they help to form a unified whole of it in that they are a kind of recapitulation of what has preceded. We can see in them the same technical mastery, themes, attitudes, and moods. In them Banville is still preoccupied by the theme of the poet's mission and place in life, presenting him as an exile and sufferer. As in Les Exilés the poet is a preserver of the gods. "Car les Dieux ne seront pas morts / Tant qu'il restera des poètes" (For the gods will not be dead as long as there are poets), he concludes in "Pessimisme" (Sonnailles et Clochettes). In "Soleil couchant" (Dans la Fournaise) the sunset symbolizes a kind of Götterdämmerung, a twilight of the gods on the point of death. But one among them stands out, white and luminous, radiating gentleness and love. Here we see again a reflection of Banville's faith in Christ. Christ intervenes directly in "L'Enfant" (Dans la Fournaise), which is really an allegory of human life with its evils and the promise of salvation seen through Christian eyes. The poem begins with a scene showing happy children at play in the Luxembourg Gardens on a clear July morning. Gradually the atmosphere becomes threatening as various specters appear--Murder, Theft, Usury, Debauchery, Avarice, Intoxication, Anger--addressing the children as follows:

> Vous serez des hommes et des femmes,

> Nés de la fange, par le désir entraînés,
> Abjects, vains; c'est pourquoi vous nous
>   appartenez.
> Ivres et furieux, vous chercherez vos joies
> Dans la chair pantelante, et vous êtes nos
>   proies.

(You will be men and women, born in slime, carried away by desire, abject, empty; that is why you belong to us. Drunk and full of fury, you will seek your pleasures in the panting flesh, and you are our prey.)

At that moment a child crowned with thorns appears. Before the limpid clarity of his eyes the specters flee and the child says to the other children, "Jouez en paix, mes petits frères" (Play in peace, my little brothers).

Many of the aspects associated with his funambulist poetry are also present in Banville's last collections. The mixture of incongruous elements is one of them. Sometimes the effect is almost surrealistic. In "Scientifique" (Sonnailles et Clochettes), for example, nymphs appear in a Romantic moonlight setting to tell the poet that the music of the zephyrs is really the voice of spring speaking through phonographs. Familiar style, occasional use of English words, verbal surprises, and rich rhymes often forming puns are some other features we have encountered before. His enjambements are, if anything, even more daring, the break occurring in such situations as the following: between stanzas, within a title ("Revue / Des deux Mondes"), within a numeral ("trois / Cent soixante-quinze"), between adverbs ("si / Vite"), between the article and its noun ("la / Lune"), or even within a word ("jus- / Qu'à"). Buffoonery and wit are also present.

It may be recalled that in the preface of Les Stalactites Banville spoke of a project of rhythmic experimentation based on familiar tunes. He comes back to this idea in Dans la Fournaise with several poems, the best of which is probably "Variations." The poet calls upon a violinist to play variations on the air "Au Clair de la lune," and the poem is thus a transposition into verbal rhythms and sonorities of the violinist's evocation of the song, which is itself suggestive of a moonlit landscape. The idea of musical variations played by the violin is paralleled by the varying reflections of the moonlight emphasized by the light of the loved one's eyes, themselves compared to heavenly bodies. The phrase "clair de la lune" or "au clair de la lune" occurs no fewer than ten times in the page-long poem in a number of rhythmical variations, so that the words "au," "la," and "lune" all become rhyme words at one time or another. The weaving of this expression into the musical fabric of the poem recalls the repetitions of "nous n'irons plus au bois" and "les lauriers sont coupés" in the poem "Nous n'irons plus au bois" (*Les Stalactites*).

Autobiographical references, though rare, sometimes add a welcome freshness to this late poetry, especially since they are usually presented in a modest and occasionally humorous manner. "Birbe" (*Sonnailles et Clochettes*) is a good example of good-natured self-deprecation. In it Banville pokes fun at his bald head, which he compares to a peeled fruit, a plucked bird, a smooth ocean rock, or a billiard ball. He then refers to his beret, which he wore constantly in later years to cover his baldness. But his poetic calling compensates for his baldness, "Car avec ou sans chevelure / Un bon chanteur n'est jamais laid" (For with or without hair a good singer is never ugly). He ends the poem by explaining that his baldness is essential so that the Muse can find room to place a laurel wreath on his skull.

While, on the whole, these three collections are not Banville's best, many a poem in them is redeemed by the poet's grace. What reader could resist the charm of a poem like "Lapins" (*Sonnailles et Clochettes*)? Who can suppress a good-humored smile and who can fail to find these little rabbits adorable after reading their little speech in which they tell us in a sophisticated way how unsophisticated they are? "Nous sommes les petits Lapins, / Gens étrangers à l'écriture" (We are the little rabbits, people foreign to writing), they announce. They reject Stendhal, Kant, Dostoievski, and Schopenhauer but adore the naturalness of La Fontaine. Their affirmation of the sheer joy of being alive as they sit "sur leurs petits derrières" (on their little behinds) reminds us of Banville's own outlook and the brightness of so much of his poetry.

Chapter Six

The Dramatist

Theories

Banville's preoccupation with theater can be traced to his boyhood when he was a student at the Pension Sabatier. As we saw earlier, the mimes of the Grimacier and the plays at the Anciens Funambules, the Théâtre Joly, and the Petit Lazari awakened in him a fascination and admiration for theater that proved to be lifelong. His reflections on the nature of theater began early, and even as a boy his critical perceptiveness was remarkable for his age. Later, as the drama critic for Le National from 1869 to 1881, he communicated to his readers on a regular basis his views on various aspects of theater. These views did not change radically, and his personal conception of drama is clear and unequivocal. He did not regard himself as a reformer; nothing new needed to be introduced because models close to his conception already existed in the plays of Shakespeare, some of the Greek playwrights, Racine, Corneille, and even Victor Hugo.

The first condition of theater for Banville is lyricism, and in this sense his plays constitute a continuation of his poetry rather than a distinct world apart from it. He does not see clear-cut frontiers between lyric poetry and drama. He is convinced that modern theater must eventually realize the necessity of combining dramatic dialogue with song and with the ode as Greek drama did. Theater has grown out of the ode, the ancestor of verbal music: "At first it was only to let the chorus have a bit of rest that its songs were cut by a recitative uttered by a character, and thus the Ode is the essential generator of dramatic poetry. It represents the impulse of our soul toward the divine and toward external nature; and as long as it is a part of comedy, whether it keeps its absolute form or whether it is only represented by Lyricism expressed in verse or in prose, comedy is complete and living" (1). Far from regarding the chorus or other lyrical elements as incidental, Banville seems to be suggesting that these are the very essence and that dramatic dialogue is of lesser importance. His conception of the primacy of lyricism or music presupposes that all other elements must be subordinate and that as far as possible the drama should be constructed by musical means. It may be recalled that as early as 1846 Banville wrote "Le Jugement de Paris," a poem in Le Sang de la Coupe, as an experiment to show how different rhythms could be used and combined according to the various characters and situations.

His views on theater often emerge from his pronouncements on the theater of his day. Melodrama, historical drama, the thesis play, Realism, local color--all of these were part of the theatrical scene during his life, and all of these he criticizes. He condemns the popular theater of Scribe, the melodrama, much Realistic theater, and historical drama because they are not human. In a sense he is condemning the type of play advocated by Diderot. We are not interested in specific situations, conditions, and professions, nor in the frivolous and transitory outward trappings of the day, he argues. Rather, we are interested in human emotions, in characters having a general, necessary, and absolute existence (2). Historical drama runs the risk of being submerged in the particulars of history, thereby diminishing the stature of characters and events. Only by subordinating historical accuracy to popular conceptions of historical characters, who in any event tend to become legendary, can the playwright hope to achieve success. Needless to say, these arguments are echoes of Aristotle and of many dramatic theorists of the sixteenth and seventeenth centuries in France.

As for the thesis play, Banville objects to it on artistic grounds, stating that "thought should circulate through the action of a drama like the blood in our veins, and it must not be served as something apart" (3). In any case, he maintains, the public often understands the opposite of what the author intended. Realistic drama is often "a flat and sterile imitation of life" (4). But a second and more important objection is expressed in Banville's column of March 16, 1874, in Le National. It is the exaggeration of man's ugliness and base nature, "for as low as he may have fallen, degraded, hideous, fierce, serving as a plaything of the most ignoble appetites, man still has on his brow a divine ray, and in his soul an unconscious desire for immortal beauty, and it is not true to show him formed out of mud only, for he has been shaped out of mud and out of light." No matter how cruel, unjust, ungrateful, or frivolous mankind is made to appear by a writer such as Aristophanes, the chorus often expresses the most lofty and divine feelings through its poetry.

Banville's view of man as a dualistic being is the fundamental reason for his insistence on lyrical theater. He regards lyricism almost as a panacea capable of saving theater from most of its errors. The greatest of these is not to take into account the divine part of man's being. Perhaps this is especially true of comedy: "Buffoonery or the comic, that is to say, the representation of man the animal, imitating his vices and his appetites, turns our stomachs with disgust, if along with these images of our flesh clinging to the gutter, we do not see the image of our soul, eager for heaven, and clamoring for it in a supernatural and divine language" (5). Some of the greatest playwrights--Aristophanes, Shakespeare, Racine, Corneille, Hugo--have provided such examples. Even Realistic plays can be saved by verse, which will allow us to bear the ugliness of reality. Historical drama also becomes possible, as Hugo has shown, through verse, which can lend elevation and greatness to characters limited by their historical particularity.

In Banville's opinion the Romantics' obsession with local color was an error, or at least it was wrong to try to produce it in a material or physical way. Here again it is poetry that can create the desired atmosphere: "It will make you see, in such a way that you will never doubt having seen them, the palace of the Doges of Venice, the palace of Hamlet, Prince of Denmark..." (_Le National_, December 22, 1873). However, even verse is not quite enough to make possible the choice of contemporary subjects. They are too close to us. It is true that poetry can produce an effect of distance, but in general Banville rejects modern subjects. The dual nature of man is echoed in what he perceives to be the double aim of theater, "to make us forget life and yet to represent it," for, he adds, "we cannot be interested in anything that is not life, and on the other hand we cannot be delighted if our cares are not magically dispelled and put to flight by almighty Illusion" (6).

Banville is generally sympathetic to Romantic theater. He does not view its best aspects as new, but rather as a return to the approach of Corneille, a rehabilitation of lyricism. He regards Hugo as a model not only in lyric poetry but also in theater, and his views are in many ways close to those found in the Préface de Cromwell. He admires the fusion of lyricism and tragedy in Victor Hugo, and it is his stated objective to do for comedy what Hugo had done for tragedy (7). Fortunately, Hugo had chosen tragedy, for the comic vision better conforms to Banville's temperament and general outlook on life. The combination of irony and wit with lyricism as practiced by Heine seems to Banville to be the only way to depict modern civilization (8). As a poet who holds that poets by definition are exiles and thus not free, he sees the comic approach as a way of affirming his presence in the face of those forces that have exiled him. That is surely the sense of these words uttered by Esope in the play by that name:

> Car celui qui subit les injures de l'air,
> Les coups, la faim, l'été dévorant, l'âpre hiver,
> L'année sombre, a du moins la revanche sublime
> De railler, comme il peut, tout ce qui nous opprime,
> Et c'est pourquoi l'esclave est un comédien.
> (act 1, scene 3)

(For the one who experiences the offenses of the air, blows, hunger, devouring summer, harsh winter, dark melancholy, at least has the sublime vengeance of railing as best he can against all that oppresses us, and that is why the slave is a comedian.)

A General Impression

Beginning with Le Feuilleton d'Aristophane of 1852, Banville published some seventeen plays. Except for Le Forgeron, the title of each one is followed by a designation containing the word "comédie" or "comique." Their publication dates are fairly evenly distributed over the last four decades of his life, the greatest productivity occurring in the 1880s, when he published five plays. All were written in verse except

Gringoire and the prologue of *Le Feuilleton d'Aristophane*. On the whole they are relatively short, ten of them consisting of one act. Their inspiration flows from various sources, from Greek mythology to contemporary Paris. Within this range the distribution is not even. Characters from Greek mythology and history are found in almost half of the plays, while only one is set in the Paris of his day, and even that one, *Le Feuilleton d'Aristophane*, has a connection with Greek antiquity. Between these two extremes of time we find several plays (*Gringoire*, *Florise*, *Le Cousin du Roi*) loosely rooted in the history of fifteenth- and seventeenth-century France. Several others (*Le Beau Léandre*, *Les Fourberies de Nérine*, *Le Baiser*, *Riquet à la Houppe*) take us into the more vaguely defined world of fantasy and owe much of their inspiration to Italian comedy and the fairy tales of Perrault.

Banville's theater has never been popular. Even those plays that had the greatest number of performances the year of their publication seldom reappeared on the stage. Others had to wait years for their première. Yet they are eminently readable. Like Musset, he might have designated them as *Un Spectacle dans un fauteuil* (A Spectacle in an armchair). In fact, their refinement, lyricism, wit, and the dreamy wistfulness of some of their characters are strongly reminiscent of Musset. But the characters usually lack the psychological truth of Musset's. In some ways Banville's theater is almost an anachronism in the nineteenth century. It shows no concern for realism or exactness in documentation and observation of contemporary life as Realistic theater did; it minimizes spectacle, contrary to some Romantic plays, notably those of Hugo; it lacks the visible action, crime, and violence characterizing melodramas and some Romantic plays; and it lacks the declamatory style found in much of Hugo. It is really an intimate theater whose greatest appeal might be to a cultivated and sensitive public. If Banville had in mind the common people (not including those he considered bourgeois), whose unspoiled instinct for beauty he believed to be intact, his appeal to such a public is reduced by the sophistication of his theater. It is true that much of its buffoonery can have an instant appeal to even the most uncultivated, but the subtleties, the nuances, the numerous literary allusions and symbols must often escape the uninitiated and those whose minds are nourished largely by clichés. That Banville was eager to establish communication between audience and players is emphasized by the fact that many, if not most, of his plays close with a few lines directed to the audience, asking its indulgence for any weaknesses, paying tribute to its patience, sometimes adding a word of explanation or commentary, and even requesting applause for a specific player.

His theater is related to life in the same way as his lyric poetry and contains many of the characteristics of the latter. Almost never gloomy and somber, certainly never morbid, it radiates warmth and brightness. The reality of the earth is not absent, but it is transmuted into a poetic reality. The characters and the sense of dialogue appear natural not so much because of Banville's perception of psychological dimensions in them, but because they are true and natural in relation to the poetic world in which they exist. Designated as comédies, these plays are not necessarily humorous, although much humor is present. Their chief aim does not appear to be to correct and modify behavior by ridiculing weaknesses, although that element is not totally absent. And certainly most of the characters are not without human infirmities. Even the Olympian gods are sometimes brought down to the level of human folly and ridiculousness. Although the characters are never mired in the depths of vice, they are not always admirable. Yet they are generally acceptable and even charming. It is through the grace of rhythm and rhyme, of poetic beauty, that they rise above prosaic, earthbound reality into the dreamlike existence of another vision.

Le Feuilleton d'Aristophane

Banville's first play, Le Feuilleton d'Aristophane, prepared in collaboration with Philoxène Boyer, can be regarded as the theatrical counterpart of his Odes Funambulesques and his Occidentales. This is his only play with a largely contemporary setting, and like the two collections of poetry just mentioned it contains satire and verbal buffoonery. Banville recalls the project in this way: "In 1852, my friend Philoxène Boyer and I got the bold idea of composing a satirical comedy, a kind of Review such as are played by genre theaters, entitled Le Feuilleton d'Aristophane, in which the Athenians in the Prologue would speak in prose, while the Parisians of the Comedy would express themselves in verse with comic and unexpected rhymes, and in which alexandrines would be mixed with lyrical stanzas, sometimes serious and sometimes clownish" (9).

This review, which played at the Odéon from December 26, 1852, to January 10, 1853, is divided into three sections: a prologue, a scene in front of the curtain, and the review proper. It is the only one of Banville's plays not constructed along more conventional lines. The prologue, set in Athens in the ninetieth Olympiad, presents three important characters: Xanthias, Aristophanes' slave, an amusing valet type reminiscent of Molière's Sganarelle; Aristophanes himself; and the Muse Thalia. Aristophanes, discouraged by his loss of inspiration and by the corruption of art which he observes, announces his departure from Athens. Xanthias, more realistic and more materialistic, comments on the misery of the poet's condition, adding that he, Xanthias, would know how to exploit Aristophanes' talent financially. Thalia arrives to say she will take Aristophanes elsewhere and to another age in order to demonstrate that humanity is an inexhaustible source of inspiration and that the manifestations of its thoughts are as varied as nature. In the scene in front of the curtain Thalia, apparently addressing a Parisian audience, speaks of the role of the poet and announces the intention of the play in these terms: "Nous décrirons vos types rares, / Nous peindrons en riant vos côtés sérieux" (We shall describe your rare types, we shall depict with laughter your serious aspects).

The main part of the play is comprised of La Revue. The presentation of contemporary life as seen by a traveler from another country or another age is a well-known technique in satirical literature. In La Revue Aristophanes wakes up, dressed in modern fashion, in strange surroundings. Thalia explains that he is now in Paris, "the heaven of minds," that it is 1852, and that Paris is a kind of new Athens whose Homer is called Balzac. She further informs him that he will take his place as the journalist Vernin. Xanthias appears as his valet Piffard. Perhaps few are better placed than the journalist to observe the present scene, for it is through him that knowledge of current events is funneled to the public. Before his eyes life in its infinite variety continues to pass like a parade.

The richness and diversity of Parisian life are underlined by the large number of scenes, twenty-one in all, into which the review is divided, as well as by the number and variety of personae. The image of Paris that unfolds is much like that presented in the *Odes Funambulesques* and the *Occidentales*. Ultimately it comes down to an examination of human values, to a confrontation between materialistic and spiritual ones. The review achieves the effect of a series of debates, sometimes through the grouping of characters in twos representing opposite points of view. One of the first to call on the journalist is the painter Realista. He explains that realism means *faire laid* ("to produce ugliness"). "Everything I draw is horribly ugly!" he exclaims. At this point Painting (really a picture) comes to life and pronounces a eulogy of art that is simple and serious, eternal and immortal, whereupon Realista is expelled. Next Eglantine comes to ask support for a plan to build railways (Banville uses the word "rail-way") to places of beauty. Tabarin brings a petition to stop the demolition of Parisian monuments. The reference to Baron Haussmann's urban modernization project is obvious. The opposing point of view is presented by a nameless street urchin who favors urban renewal because of his "love of the modern era."

After this there is a confrontation between l'Imprimerie ("Printing") and King Midas. L'Imprimerie accuses Midas of besmirching his sacred art, while Midas replies that his accuser is using his art to "reduce the value of money from which joy is born." But Vernin agrees with l'Imprimerie that "the Idea is everything." The last pair relates to music. The picture Musique becomes animated in order to extol real music, "purified sound," "the art of the great Palestrina, of Gluck and of Mozart," made for those who have tired "of terrestrial horizons." What Musique condemns is embodied by Tempesta, who represents noise or noisy percussive and brassy music, which is characterized as *tintamarre* ("racket").

In the last scene the setting is once again Athens but all the characters of the review are there also in a kind of fusion of ancient Athens and the new Athens, which is Paris. The Fée du Palais de Cristal ("fairy from the Crystal Palace") appears out of the earth and exhorts the world, and especially France, to greater progress. The play closes with a sonnet ingeniously arranged as a dialogue between Aristophanes and Thalia, complimenting the audience and expressing the wish that players and playwright may have given it pleasure.

Le Feuilleton d'Aristophane is almost entirely lacking in plot, in depth of characterization, and in logical motivation. Banville is not concerned about presenting life as the Realists of his day tried to do. Nor is his aim to achieve complete verisimilitude. Life for him is full of miracles; they are the norm. After all, what is so surprising about a fairy rising out of the earth or pictures coming to life? The main point is that his ingenious technique of showing modern life through the perspective of the journalist enables him to present the changing panorama of Parisian life together with editorial comment. Furthermore, the translation of Aristophanes to Paris underlines once again his dream of recapturing for modern life some of the values he admired in Greek antiquity.

Comic Effects

Although the dividing line between comedy and seriousness in Banville's theater is not always clearly drawn, the most pervasive tone of his plays is that of good-humored, wholesome gayety. Banville has at his command a wide range of comic effects, from slapstick humor and puns to sophisticated literary allusion, from farce and buffoonery to subtle wordplay. Perhaps Columbine's words to the audience at the close of *Le Beau Léandre* best characterize that flavor: "When the Muse with clear laughter shakes rhyme, that sword with magic flashes, and when she comes to you her forehead stained with dregs, with vines running down, and dressed as a fool, let her have her gayety even in such excess, for her immortal laughter is French common sense" (*le bon sens français*).

This *bon sens français*, while lacking some of the earthiness and irreverence of what is sometimes known as *l'esprit gaulois*, is nonetheless related to it. Banville's first play borrows as its main character the greatest of Greek comedy writers, Aristophanes. The French roots of Banville's comedy go back to medieval fabliaux and farces and find nourishment along the way in the tradition of Italian comedy and Molière. Even some of his more serious plays bear traces of this heritage. For example, in Florise, most of whose characters are members of a wandering company of players, we find the name Jodelet, a name already well known from the Commedia dell'Arte and Molière's Les Précieuses ridicules. This highly sensitive and delightful character, this innocent dreamer, is treated as a fool by his comrades, who provide an element of slapstick comedy by beating him with handkerchiefs. Socrate et sa femme, not based on an inherently comical subject, manages to resurrect the theme of the mal marié ("unhappily married") so often found in medieval fabliaux and farces.

In some of Banville's most humorous plays, especially those inspired by Molière and the Commedia dell' Arte, we can identify another important ancestor, La Farce de Maître Pathelin. Their characters are ignoble and, as in Pathelin, each tries to trick the others. Les Fourberies de Nérine is reminiscent of Molière's Les Fourberies de Scapin. In a monologue opening Banville's play Scapin reveals that Géronte has died and that he wants to go away with Géronte's worldly possessions stuffed into a huge sack, leaving Nérine behind. Nérine, overhearing the monologue and wishing to marry this elusive bachelor, persuades Scapin, through a wily ruse, to climb into the sack where he claims to have put Géronte. She hastily ties it and begins to beat him. After cutting his way out he tells her of Zaïda, who, he says, loves him madly. Thereupon Nérine takes his knife and pretends to kill herself. Not taken in by the ruse, he now realizes that she loves him and he consents to marry her.

In Le Beau Léandre we find three wily characters, fairly evenly matched. Léandre can marry Orgon's daughter Columbine only if he pays Orgon one hundred crowns. An expert in obtaining money from beautiful women, Léandre attempts to get the necessary amount from Columbine herself. She is not fooled, but she wants to marry him. This leads to an effective comic scene in which all three stand in a row. Orgon asks Léandre for the money, he in turn asks Columbine, and she completes the circle by asking her father. When everyone understands the situation, Orgon decides to give his daughter to Léandre without the money, but Léandre gives her back. Columbine finds herself pushed back and forth between her father and lover like a shuttlecock between two racquets. Finally she succeeds in talking Léandre into marrying her by revealing the location of Orgon's hidden treasure, which everyone except Léandre knows is no longer there.

This kind of trickery is not confined to mortals. Even the gods practice it and even excel in it. Mercury, in La Pomme, refers to himself as "le roi superbe des filous" (the superb king of tricksters). He is in love with Hebe, who spurns him. She has, however, promised to be more receptive to him if he will obtain Venus's magic girdle for Juno, who wishes to win back the unfaithful Jupiter. The unusual property of the girdle is that it makes the wearer irresistible. In Venus, Mercury meets a formidable opponent, almost as shrewd and skilled in deceit as he is. She thinks she has won a victory in persuading him to part with a tempting apple that he is to deliver to Jupiter's newest conquest. But we find that it is only bait that allows him to take possession of her girdle. In the end the girdle is not needed, for Juno and Jupiter have been reconciled, and Venus learns that the apple with which Mercury seemed so reluctant to part is not the only one in his possession. As a messenger of the gods his role is akin to that of a valet. He is a kind of nineteenth-century Figaro. Like Figaro, he is a skillful valet and derives pleasure from outwitting those whom he serves. In his opening monologue, where he gives an amusing impersonation of the voices of those who send him on errands, together with his replies, there are unmistakable echoes of the famous "Largo al Factotum" of Rossini's operatic Figaro:

> --Ho! Mercure!
> --Hein? -- Mercure par-ci. -- Quoi? -- Mercure par-là.
> En haut! En bas! Partout! Las ou non, me voilà.
>
> (v. 9, p. 224)

(Hey, Mercury! -- Eh? -- Mercury here! -- What? -- Mercury there. Up above! Down below! Everywhere! Tired or not, there I am.)

There is always a risk that liars, cheats, and thieves may become odious to the public. This is not so in Banville's theater. The clowning that is a part of all these rascals makes them not only acceptable but entertaining and likable. Many of them are young; their freshness and zest for life, not to speak of the beauty of the verse in which they speak, transport them into a world governed by the laws of rhyme and rhythm and make us forget that they are ignoble by earthly standards.

In addition to comedy of character, Banville produces comic effects similar to those in his lyric poetry, some of which depend on skillful use of language. His penchant for drawing amusement from puns, most often at the rhyme, is again noticeable. For example, when Mercury tries to impress on Venus the possible serious consequences for him for having let her have the apple, he says:

> Il se peut que, malgré mes soupirs éloquents,
> Je sois, comme Vulcain, jeté sous des volcans,
> Ou que, m'assimilant à Phébus, on m'admette
> A garder les moutons comme lui, chez Admète!
> (v. 9, p. 250)

> (It is possible that, in spite of my eloquent sighs, I may be thrown, like Vulcan, beneath volcanoes, or that, assimilating myself with Phoebus, I may be admitted to take care of the sheep, like him, for Admetus.)

Needless to say, the translation into English does not reflect sufficiently well the puns Vulcain-volcans and m'admette-Admète.

Puns and unusual rhymes may be regarded as a particular case of a more general technique dear to Banville, that of unexpected or even incongruous combinations or associations. Let us consider for a moment the play Le Baiser. The stage directions tell us that its setting is the Viroflay woods and that the time is now. In spite of this, we are thrown into a timeless and fanciful world in which fairies and miraculous transformations are the norm. We cannot feel that the setting is France and that the time is now. The result is that the unexpected reference to credit and bailiffs, a perfectly normal reflection of an important aspect of modern bourgeois life, seems incongruous. Similarly, when Mercury calls Juno's thunderclap "a bizarre use of the official style," we think immediately of official bureaucratic jargon in the middle of a play whose setting is Cytherea and whose characters are mythological gods.

At times the incongruousness stems from a contrast in styles. Pierrot and the fairy Urgèle, in Le Baiser, express the rapture of their love and the prospect of their wedded bliss in verses of great tenderness and delicacy, into which Pierrot injects the line, "Nous nous adorerions sans cesse, énormément" (We would adore each other unceasingly, enormously). The colloquial "énormément" is not consistent with the delicate poetry of most of the scene and gives it a humorous or at least an amusing turn. Who could resist a smile at this passage as their love scene continues:

Urgèle
Nous serons blancs tous deux.
(We shall both be white.)
Pierrot
Blancs comme l'avalanche.
(White as the avalanche).
Urgèle
Blancs comme le glacier qui s'irise et qui penche.
(White as the iridescent and sloping glacier.)
Pierrot
Blancs comme Eglé qui dort auprès d'un sien ami.
(White as Eglé sleeping close to a friend.)
Urgèle
Blancs comme des cheveux d'académicien.
(White as the hair of an academician.)
Pierrot
Tout avait conspiré pour que je t'adorasse.
(Everything had conspired that I might adore you.)
(v. 6, p. 291)

What begins as an idyllic and poetic evocation leads first through repetition and then, in the comparison with the white hair of an academician, to a sudden change of imagistic quality. The reference to the academician suggests the idea of a certain stiff erudition summed up in the pompous and nonpoetic imperfect subjunctive "adorasse," not to speak of the utterly incongruous association between the historically defined French Academy and the poetically elusive and undefined fairy-tale setting. On the other hand, in the same play, gratuitous references to Rothschild, the stock exchange, a trip to Senlis, or even to the filous ("crooks") of the United States prevent our taking too seriously the world of fantasy.

Another source of amusement is Banville's use of literary allusion and pastiche. Here again Le Baiser provides some of the best examples. If we recall the scene in which Molière's Tartuffe tries to seduce Elmire we can appreciate the following speeches, mostly by Pierrot, as he and Urgèle speak of their love and their plans for marriage:

Pierrot

Mon innocence commence enfin à me peser,
Et, pour être Pierrot, je n'en suis pas moins homme.
(My innocence is finally beginning to be a burden, and even though I am Pierrot I am nonetheless a man.)

Urgèle

Ah! Tout beau! Que fait là votre main?
(Not so fast! What is your hand doing there?)

Pierrot

Je tâte votre habit, l'étoffe en est...
(I am feeling your clothing, the material is...)
(v. 6, p. 287)

A little later, when Urgèle is on the point of giving in to Pierrot, she asks him to look around to make certain no one is spying on them. He replies, "Baste! A quoi bon? Ces bois sont aveugles et sourds..." (Nonsense! What for? These woods are blind and deaf). Like Elmire, Urgèle insists, and when Pierrot returns, he echoes Molière's Tartuffe with the words, "Madame, tout conspire à mon contentement" (Madam, everything conspires toward my satisfaction). This elaborate pastiche amuses because, whereas in the mouth of Tartuffe the words are sinister, no one really takes Pierrot seriously. When Urgèle's comrades, the other fairies, call her to rejoin them, she does so, leaving Pierrot to reflect that he will never again see her. "Nevermore," he says, employing the English term of Edgar Allan Poe. Briefly he contemplates suicide, echoing Hamlet's words: "Mais, en effet, doit-on voir Pierrot pendu? -- L'être, / Ou ne pas l'être, c'est la question" (But really, should Pierrot be seen hanged? -- To be [hanged] or not to be, that is the question). But he quickly resolves the question, concluding, "Je veux effroyablement vivre" (I have a frightfully strong desire to live).

Noble Ideals

While not all of Banville's plays are humorous, the world in which his characters move tends to be sunlit and removed from the prosaic realities of contemporary life or, for that matter, of any age. The fact that almost all of his plays are set in a distant past, historical, legendary, or even fanciful, can be seen as a translation of his nostalgia for an even more distant paradise and man's state of pre-exile. The physical or visual setting as indicated by Banville at the beginning of some of his more fanciful plays is more than a little suggestive of Eden. Its components are ageless trees, mossy stones, and crystalline springs, all bathed in the light of dawn. This is the kind of setting we find in *Riquet à la Houppe* and *Le Baiser*, both peopled with fairies. Even more than these two, *Diane au bois* is set in a world of virginal freshness and purity, geographically located near Mount Olympus but nonetheless evoking paradisiacal beginnings. It could be argued that the setting of *Diane au bois* is not just a backdrop for the plot but is in reality part of the subject of the play. The chaste goddess Diana, courted by Eros, proves in the end not to be immune to the charms of love after all. The beauty of this love is interwoven with the freshness and pristine state of nature so that the whole play is a kind of hymn to the purity of love and nature, each enhancing the other. But this world is "such stuff / As dreams are made on," as Eros tells the public in an epilogue filled with Shakespearean accents:

> Rêver aux mois d'été sous les rameaux flottants,
> Dans le grand palais vert de la nature fée,
> Croire que l'on entend au loin l'archet d'Orphée,
> N'est-ce pas le meilleur d'un monde où tout
> n'est rien?
> Or, notre comédie au voile aérien
> Est un songe entrevu dans le bois de délices
> Où le lys éploré regarde les calices

Des étoiles, avant cette heure où l'aube naît
Dans la brume d'opale....
(v. 9, p. 68)

(To dream in May months beneath the floating boughs in the great green palace of the fairy world, to imagine one hears the bow of Orpheus in the distance, is that not the best part of a world where all is nothing? Now, our comedy with its airy veil is a dream glimpsed in the woods of delight where the tearful lily looks at the calyxes of the stars before the hour when dawn is born in the opal mist.)

Idyllic settings constitute part of the dream and quest of many Banvillean characters. To live in a land removed from prosaic and bourgeois pavements corresponds to their vision of an ideal state. The character with the title role in the play _Florise_ clearly communicates this aspiration as she contemplates the park, which is the setting of the play. For her, it is a "divine landscape" with its ageless and gigantic trees, its flowers, its medieval castle, its murmuring fountains, its marble statues, and its singing brooks. Its enchantment and peace are such "that one would wish to live and die here, lulled by the song of these brooks."

A striking harmony exists between such settings and most of the important characters in Banville's more serious plays. These characters would be hopelessly out of place in the prosaic world of everyday living, and in this sense they can be said to be exiles. Some of them are gods and some are fairies, perfectly in tune with the idyllic setting as in _Riquet à la Houppe_ and _Le Baiser_. But the majority are human beings, most of whom are writers, actors, and legendary heroes. What distinguishes them is their sensitivity, their nobility of soul, and their joyful acceptance of sacrifice and duty. There is about them an innocence corresponding to the freshness of the settings in which they find themselves.

One of the oldest among the writers is Aesop, a slave physically deformed but spiritually superior. But he is misunderstood. Rhodope, another slave, loved by King Cresus, but herself in love with Aesop, attempts to explain to the king the nature of Aesop's fables, in terms that might also describe Banville's theater: they are narratives, sometimes comical and graceful, in which the naked truth appears and in which the elements of nature speak in their turn. The vast universe which files by our eyes teaches us courage, faith, love, and sacrifice, while forcing us to face our vices as in a mirror (act 1, scene 3). In return for special services to the king, Aesop is set free and allowed to request anything he wishes. At this point he departs, making a supreme sacrifice by not asking for Rhodope. For him, one of the more somber characters in Banville's theater, there is consolation only in death: "Et la femme est bizarre et l'homme n'est pas beau, / Le repos tant cherché n'est que dans le tombeau" (And woman is bizarre and man is not beautiful. Rest, so much longed for, can be found only in the grave).

Two other misunderstood poets are Gringoire and Dufresny in Gringoire and Le Cousin de Roi, respectively. The former is called a "wicked and dangerous child" like all the other rhymers, who "are madmen running loose," while one of the courtiers in Le Cousin du Roi speaks of the poet's disdain for the ordinary things of life. But in both plays the poet's role is exalted by the poets themselves and by the women who love them. According to Gringoire the poet suffers the griefs of others and gives them a voice. Dufresny sees the poet as an outcast, "a beggar everywhere disinherited," while Angélique, who loves him, regards the poet as a prophet and teacher. Dufresny, the impractical dreamer, helpless as a child in the world of hard realities, is Banville's version of Vigny's Chatterton, while Angélique automatically recalls Kitty Bell. However, both Dufresny and Gringoire find happiness in love and both are able to enjoy the protection of the king. But this is not how life really is for poets; it is a fiction. "O public, notre histoire est un conte de fées" (Oh audience, our story is a fairy tale), says Angélique to the spectators.

Apart from his comic figures, most of Banville's major characters are dominated by a vision or an ideal transcending material concerns, making them in a sense "otherworldly" and leaving the impression that they can be completely real only in a better world. For Socrates, life is a quest for truth (Socrate et sa femme). In Déïdamia Achilles, forced to decide whether to accept Ulysses' order to meet Hector in combat, is in reality confronted with the age-old choice between security and possibly cowardice on the one hand, and danger and heroism on the other. Duty and honor triumph. He leaves mother, wife, and son. He is an exile too, condemned to greatness, one of those for whom, according to his wife, glory is the only good and the fatherland the only wife.

The women are a fitting match for the men: Déïdamia, beautiful, eloquent, a person of great dignity and noble bearing, accepts the choice made by her husband Achilles, sacrificing her own domestic happiness; Florise remains true to her duty as an actress, placing it ahead of private satisfactions; and the goddess Diana is dominated by the ideal of chastity, accepting only the purest and most elevated love. Rhodope, Angélique, and Loyse (in Gringoire) are all women of distinction, chaste, devoted to the poets they love, selfless, and in all matters worthy of the men they love.

These portraits are of course unusual; they are embodiments of Banville's ideal of womanhood. But the question of love and women in his theater is not without ambiguity. Aesop, as we have seen, regards women as bizarre. Socrates' wife Xantippe tells the audience that all evil has come from women: "Clouded reasoning, the appetite for wealth, treason, golden cups in which wines are mixed with dregs, all crime, all happy lies, all madness, come from her." But Socrates adds, "Adore her anyway, since it is the gods who have created her, and she is still the best part of their creation." Mercury, in La Pomme, sees her as the eternally tempted and tempting, "For as long as red fruit will ripen, woman will want to bite into it, and as long as we exist, we shall always love her who eats apples."

As for love, many of Banville's plays dwell on its transforming power, especially that of beautifying and ennobling. In Le Baiser Urgèle, changed into an ugly old woman by a sorcerer, can be released from her spell only by a kiss from an innocent young man who has never kissed anyone before. Pierrot, who has those qualifications, reluctantly gives her a kiss, and to his amazement sees her transformed into a fairy of dazzling beauty and youth, robed in a moon-colored dress. The miraculous power of love is an important theme in Riquet à la Houppe also. King Myrtil, whose fortunes have suffered a severe decline, is desperately looking for a wealthy suitor for his daughter Rose, who is beautiful but mindless. The fairy Diamant has a godson Riquet, who would be an eligible suitor if only he had better looks to go with his wit and wealth. Diamant decides with Rose's godmother, the fairy Cyprine, to arrange a meeting between Riquet and Rose. Rose has only to say to him, "Je t'aime," and he will be handsome. Riquet needs only to love Rose and she will become intelligent. The meeting takes place and the anticipated miracle occurs. But was it really a miracle, or was it an illusion, allowing lovers to see only the beautiful in each other? That is a possibility that Riquet considers:

> Pourtant je serai beau, si ma chère princesse
> Peut me voir ainsi, car l'Illusion sans cesse
> Nous transfigure, et sait d'un oiseau très banal
> Faire ce merle blanc qu'on nomme l'idéal.
> (v. 4, p. 271)

> (Still I shall be handsome if my dear princess can see me that way, for Illusion transfigures us ceaselessly and can make out of a very ordinary bird that rare bird called the ideal.)

Protagonists in other plays are strengthened and ennobled in varying degrees through love. Perhaps Dufresny best sums up its virtue when he says that love has made him simple and good and has caused him to be born again.

Florise

If love ranks high among the ideals of Banville, it is clear that art ranks even higher. Art has its elect who suffer for it. It is a world apart and those who inhabit it will forever be unconsoled exiles among ordinary mortals. *Florise*, one of Banville's longer plays, is his most substantial treatment in dramatic form of the artist's condition. Dating from 1870 and labeled a comedy in four acts, *Florise* transports the reader into a poetic atmosphere. The notation at the beginning that the action is situated at the Château d'Atys near Blois in 1600 does nothing to make us feel that the play is rooted in a world we know. Nor does the presence of the historically real playwright Alexandre Hardy as one of the main characters reassure us in this regard. But that is not a fault, for one of the virtues of the play is that it allows us to live for a time in another world, in which art and, to a lesser degree, love are sovereign.

The play is preceded by an argument in the form of a quatrain from Victor Hugo's well-known "Tristesse d'Olympio":

> Toutes les passions s'éloignent avec l'âge,
> L'une emportant son masque et l'autre son
> couteau,
> Comme un essaim chantant d'histrions en
> voyage
> Dont le groupe décroît derrière le coteau.

> (All passions go away with age, one taking away its mask and another its knife like a group of actors singing as they travel and fading from sight beyond the hill.)

When the play opens Célidée and her nephew Olivier receive a company of actors headed by the playwright Hardy and including the principal actress Florise. Hardy loves Florise but she and Olivier love each other. As the actors are preparing to perform a scene from *L'Amazone Hippolyte*, Florise undergoes an internal struggle between her temptation to leave the stage in order to stay with Olivier and her compelling need to be true to herself as an artist. To Olivier she says:

> Je suis la lyre aux sons divers que le poète
> Fait résonner et qui sans lui serait muette,
> Une comédienne, enfin. Je ne suis pas
> Une femme....
>
> (v. 9, p. 157)

> (I am the lyre from which the poet draws varied sounds and which without him would be silent, an actress, in short. I am not a woman.)

But to Hardy she declares that she is a woman knowing real emotion. Hardy envisages a symbolic union:

> Nous avions fait ce rêve, ô ma beauté
> sereine,

De vivre embrassés, mais purs de la fange humaine;
Nous voulons, affranchis de ce délire obscur
Des passions, garder nos yeux emplis d'azur
Et nous unir, non dans la chair, mais par l'idée!
(v. 9, pp. 190-91)

(We had had this dream, oh my serene beauty, of living in an embrace but free of human mire. Freed from that dark delirium of passions, we wanted to keep our eyes filled with azure and to be united, not in the flesh, but through the idea!)

Florise readily admits this dream but Hardy's ideal love frightens and confuses her. She decides to abandon the stage, but when the actress replacing her performs in a mediocre fashion, Florise can restrain herself no longer. She takes over the role herself, and with this gesture comes the realization that art is for her a world superior to love. She has found her true self. The stage, she tells Olivier, is reality, and it was during her brief sojourn in Olivier's world that she was acting. She cannot leave her fellow players, she is one with them, she hears the clarion call of the Muse, and she and Olivier will not find common ground, for she and her likes are exiles in his world:

L'art est une patrie aux grands cieux éclatants
Où vivent, en dehors des pays et des temps,
Les élus qu'il choisit pour ses vivantes proies;
Et ceux-là, donnez-leur vos demeures, vos joies,
Tous les honneurs, toujours leurs coeurs inconsolés
Pleureront, car ils sont chez vous des exilés!
(v. 9, p. 212)

(Art is a land of wide shining skies where dwell, outside of countries and times, the elect whom it has chosen as its living prey; and to them give your dwellings, your joys, all honors; always their unconsoled hearts will weep, for they are exiles in your world.)

Hardy sees the artist's life as a relentless struggle. He hears the call of duty urging him on to sacrifice and effort, and in the end, when death comes, the value of his life will be measured by his devotion to his ideal. Whether he wins or loses, "to confess one's belief" is to have lived; "that is what makes us divine," he concludes.

In the sense that all the actors, as artists, are exiles, _Florise_ comes closest to being the dramatic counterpart of _Les Exilés_. Florise speaks not only for herself but for art. The play is largely an allegory of life. The players arrive at dawn, perform, and depart over the crest of the hill at sunset. As the actors fade into the distance, Célidée explains the parallel to Olivier:

> La vie! -- Elle ressemble à ce jour, dont tu vois
> Tomber le soir tremblant sur la cime des bois!
> Au matin, sous la douce aurore qui l'effleure,
> Le fier jeune homme voit venir vers sa demeure
> Les Illusions, puis l'Amour, l'Espoir vermeil,
> Et les Passions, groupe adorable et pareil
> A ces gais histrions qui, la lèvre entr'ouverte,
> Sont descendus vers nous de la colline verte!
> . . . .
> Mais lorsque le soir vient, quand le jeune homme
> est vieux,
> . . . .
> Il reste face à face avec la Solitude,
> Et voit passer, conduits par l'antique Destin,
> Sur le même coteau ses hôtes du matin,
> Mais lassés et vieillis, _l'un emportant son_
> _masque_
> _Et l'autre son couteau_....
>
> (v. 9, p. 217)

(Life! It resembles this day whose evening light you see trembling over the treetops. In the morning, beneath the gentle dawn which touches him, the proud young man sees coming toward his dwelling Illusion, then Love, scarlet Hope, and Passions, an adorable group and similar to those gay actors who with half-open lips came down to us from the green slopes.... But when evening comes, when the young man is old... he remains face to face with Solitude, and sees passing on the same hill, led by ancient Destiny, his guests of the morning, but wearied and aged, one carrying away his mask and the other his dagger.)

What is especially remarkable about all these "exiles" and about Banville's characters generally is their serenity and their willing acceptance of their condition. We search in vain for signs of inner anguish, of revolt, and of somber pessimism. They make their way through life with a cheerful spirit and a disposition as radiant as the verse in which they express themselves.

Le Forgeron

Perhaps is is in Le Forgeron that Banville gives their broadest meaning to the concepts of love and art. Dated 1887, Le Forgeron has its setting in ancient Greece on Mount Olympus and on the Aegean island of Lemnos, not long after the subjugation of Prometheus by the Olympian gods. Jupiter (Banville employs the Roman names of the gods here) has imprisoned Amor, god of love, and law rules now, not humanity, not the spirit of love. Amor, however, escapes and from his wounded flank his blood falls into the ocean, where like a seed it generates the beautiful Venus from out of the foam. Determined to maintain the dominance of law over love, Jupiter orders Venus to choose a husband for herself before nightfall. Three suitors present themselves: Bacchus, Apollo, and Jupiter himself. The first has the cup, the second the lyre, and the third thunder.

Refusing all three, Venus asks to be taken to the blacksmith Vulcan, who has made the cup, the lyre, and the thunderbolt. She is fascinated by this mysterious figure who, like Aesop and Quasimodo, is physically deformed but has a beautiful soul. Unlike her three suitors, who are untouched by human suffering, Vulcan is concerned about the welfare of human beings and devotes his labors to their betterment. When Venus understands this nobility of spirit and when, as a woman, she receives jewels made especially for her by Vulcan, she decides to marry him.

It is true that Banville takes liberties with Greek mythology here. Amor is treated like Prometheus, and the blood from his mutilation recalls Uranos. Vulcan, the jailor of Prometheus, at the same time adopts the role of Prometheus as a civilizer of mankind. But Banville is less concerned with historical accuracy than with the symbolic value of his characters. His interest in ancient Greece stems partly from the fact that he admires in it a certain gentleness in which he sees a forerunner of Christian morality (10).

This morality and these values are represented by Venus and Vulcan, and their union is characterized by Vulcan as "the loving marriage of work and creative force." It is thus symbolic. Venus is not only the incarnation of love, but also the very soul of the world, "la grande âme des choses," as Diana says. Her love is all-embracing and her pity goes out to man whom she recognizes as an exile "toujours maudit et châtié" (v. 2, p. 243) (constantly cursed and punished). Vulcan speaks of himself as "l'exilé de la nuit et de l'ombre" (v. 2, p. 274) (the exile of night and shadow). Like other Banvillean exiles, he is haunted by visions and dreams of beauty and harmony. He also loves and pities man, and he is an artist in the broad sense of making beautiful objects for the elevation of the human condition. Together he and Venus will bring light into a dark world. Vulcan calls on man to remain great "par l'appétit du ciel" (v. 2, p. 289) (through the appetite for heaven), and closes the play with the wish that in spite of fierce destiny and blind law the human race might flourish through his union with Venus. This symbolic union may well sum up Banville's vision of a life whose essence is composed of love, beauty, and creativity.

Chapter Seven

The World of Fiction

Banville's "Comédie humaine"

Banville's works in verse, already substantial, are surpassed in volume by his prose. His prose fiction, scarcely mentioned in most histories of French literature, remains largely unexplored territory. Yet after 1880 he devoted himself mostly to prose writing and between this date and his death published at least a dozen volumes of prose, most of which first appeared in Le Gil Blas. Not all of this was fiction. His Lettres chimériques consists of forty-seven letters addressed to various contemporaries, but never delivered to them, expressing his reactions to events and writings of the time. La Lanterne magique is a volume of satirical fantasies near the end of which he announces his Camées parisiens to his readers as follows: "I am going to take my leave now as projectionist of my magic lantern; but I shall not delay my return through another door, in the form of a jeweller, maker and merchant of cameos" (1). These "cameos" are exquisite miniatures, portraits of contemporary figures. Still other volumes--Paris vécu, Feuilles volantes, L'Ame de Paris--consist of miscellaneous articles on subjects of the day and reflecting Parisian life. Similar to these, but superior and probably better known, is the collection of articles, notes, and portraits entitled Mes Souvenirs, an invaluable document on Banville's early life, his ideas on various aspects of art, and his impressions of some of his contemporaries.

His prose fiction fills eight volumes. The last of these is a novel entitled Marcelle Rabe, while the other seven contain nearly three hundred short stories grouped under the following titles: Contes pour les femmes, Contes féeriques, Contes héroïques, Contes bourgeois, Dames et Demoiselles, Les Belles Poupées, and Madame Robert. Contes pour les femmes, Dames et Demoiselles, and Madame Robert are devoted largely to the theme of love. As we might expect, tales of fantasy are to be found in Contes *féeriques*, the original title of which was *Contes fantastiques*. Stories of violence predominate in *Contes héroïques*, presenting extraordinary characters and exaggerated accomplishments. *Contes bourgeois* provides an unflattering image of bourgeois life dominated by self-interest, folly, unhappiness in marriage, hypocrisy, and incomprehension of the artist. The most distinctive feature of *Les Belles Poupées* is indicated in the prologue by Chanderlos, manufacturer of dolls, who explains that each of his dolls has a story to tell, a true one, for the eyes and the face do not lie as words may lie.

In a sense Banville's "Avant-Propos" to *Contes pour les femmes* may be regarded as a foreword to his short stories as a whole. It is here that he indicates what he was hoping to achieve and why he chose the short story form. He begins by remarking that whereas life styles and settings are constantly being renewed, literary forms are limited in number and for that reason they have to be preserved and rehabilitated if they fall into disuse, as he has done for certain verse forms. He proposes to do the same for the old French *conte*:

> Today, no longer alone this time, but at the same time as other writers with a passionate interest in our origins, I am trying to restore the old French *conte*, to give an honorable place to it in our literature. It has seemed to me that with its lively and precise pace, it could marvelously well serve to represent modern life, so dense, so complicated and diverse, that it is impossible to apprehend it in large masses and that it can really only be grasped in its episodes, as in short rhapsodies, in which the innumerable skirmishes of that *Iliad* are seen and fixed on the run. (2)

Banville's reference to the *Iliad* suggests that he is thinking of life as an epic, and in the episodic approach he envisages he is very much a man of the nineteenth century. But contrary to many of his contemporaries who wrote epics consisting of numerous individual poems, Banville proposes to write in prose and to depict modern life rather than the past. However, an outstanding and monumental model for such an undertaking already existed: Balzac's *Comédie humaine*.

Indeed Banville evokes largely the same world as Balzac, attempts to situate his *milieux* with precision, and peoples his stories with characters from a variety of social strata and occupations. His ambition seems to be to produce an epic of modern Parisian life in all its complexity.

There can be little doubt that the *Comédie humaine* had made a deep impression on him. In a number of articles he expresses his admiration for Balzac, that giant of fiction. Even in Banville's short stories there are many references to him. Some of Banville's characters know Balzac and have read his work. One of the main characters in "Une Marionette" (*Contes pour les femmes*) is a novelist for whom, as for Balzac, his created characters are more real than living people. In a *dizain* opening his *Contes pour les femmes* Banville acknowledges his debt to Balzac. In "Duel des monstres" from that collection Balzac is a character who grapples with the god Proteus in order to wrest from him the secret of feminine psychology. In "Platonisme" (*Contes héroïques*) Balzac is reported as saying, "Today money is what nobility was formerly," while the following quotation from "Discrétion" (*Contes bourgeois*) might almost have come from the "Avant-Propos" of Balzac's *Comédie humaine*: ". . . for in a specific case, the refined people of civilization behave exactly like cannibalistic islanders and there is the whole secret of *La Comédie humaine*" (*Contes bourgeois*, p. 160).

Yet for all Banville's admiration of Balzac, his stories in the final analysis are not very Balzatian. His world lacks the epic stature and the intense energy of that super-reality that charcterizes Balzac's creation. Although many of Banville's characters are unusual, they are not epic heroes. Banville makes little distinction between fiction and reality, or fiction and fantasy. One blends into the other. Madame Récamier, Baudelaire, Buloz, Vieuxtemps, Sara Bernhardt, Gounod, and Gavarni move in the same world as fictitious characters and interact with them. Characters from mythology, legend, and history--Hercules, Roland, Proteus, for example--inhabit the same world and at the same time. But that is not all: fairies intermingle with people, Satan comes to sit for Gavarni, and the Demon of Perversity confronts Baudelaire, as if these events were part of everyday life. In this way Banville introduces too many characters from reality to create an autonomous fictional world, and too many elements of fantasy to produce the illusion of everyday life.

His world is almost never ordinary. Even when he tries to present everyday reality there is about it a certain "air de décor féerique" (atmosphere of a fairylike setting), as one critic puts it (3). In reply to a statement that nothing unusual happens in life Dr. Scriber in "L'Irréparable" (*Contes pour les femmes*) says, "On the contrary, only unheard of things [*des chose inouïes*] happen in it" (p. 190). Thus the reader encounters the supernatural and the uncommon at every turn: a naked statue appears and disappears, an American newspaper editor knows events before they occur, a swan sings, old women are transformed into beautiful damsels or vice versa, a fairy assumes the form of a snake, and a cat is at the same time a powder puff.

At a first reading, Banville's stories may give the feeling of richness and variety of characters and events, corresponding to what he regards as the complexity and density of modern life. The impression of diversity is reinforced at times by the introduction of relatively trivial matters. For example, the first few stories in *Contes pour les femmes* are not fiction at all, but rather essays on, or discussions of, such topics as how to escort a lady, how to receive her, or how to understand her. In reality the characters are not so numerous after all. Names may change but many of the characters remain basically the same from one story to another. The poet or other artist, the prostitute, the virtuous woman--these remain essentially unchanged regardless of name. Action and events, for all their apparent diversity, in the end serve mostly to illustrate ideas or visions, very nearly the same ones as in Banville's lyric poetry and in his theater, but perhaps somewhat more somber.

In his prose fiction, if anywhere, Banville occasionally touches the boundaries of a domain dear to the Naturalists, in which social problems such as poverty, prostitution, and alcoholism are central, but he never fully enters it. As elsewhere in his writings, he is keenly aware ot the imperfections of life, not only as they relate to the nature of man, but also as he sees them in his own age. If there were a choice, one would not choose human life. The statue Omphale in "La Lydienne" (Contes féeriques) comes to life briefly in response to the burning desire of the sculptor, but decides to return to stony immobility: "Ah, a thousand times better to return to delightful, icy oblivion in which the feeling of my existence was only an imperceptible rhythm vibrating in the infinite ecstasies of immaculate whiteness" (p. 108). "Le Villageois et le Serpent" from Fables choisies mises en prose, a collection of several fables in prose appended to Dames et Demoiselles, contains the observation that life is often "like a comedy in which the players have been badly cast" (p. 332). Banville is fond of such generalizations and many of his tales resemble prose fables in that they illustrate some moral judgment. At best, man's knowledge amounts to little enough. "We never know anything; and that is what our erudition consists of," we read in "Le Pot de terre" (Contes bourgeois, p. 282). In the epilogue of Les Belles Poupées the dollmaker maintains that the essential question is to know who will eventually triumph, courtesans or virtuous women, "for the eternal, implacable, and unceasing struggle between these two classes of persons constitutes, in sum, the whole history of humanity" (pp. 334-35).

While such a philosophy of history may not be acceptable to all, it is true that the subject of love and women is a major one in Banville's prose. Themes relating to it range from the more superficial question of etiquette, dress, and decorum to the most fundamental nature of woman and the relationship between the sexes. Discussions concerning the subtleties of love abound, not without some echoes of similar discussions in more distant periods of French literature. One dominant idea is the impossibility of perfect love on earth. In "Fagots et Fagots" (Dames et Demoiselles) the Duchesse Agnès de Cytre states that love "demands the impossible union of all luxuries and that in order not to die of satiety, it must perish painfully in some horrible and tragic catastrophe" (p. 145). The enemies of love are boredom, suspicion, jealousy, satiety, and lies; and its nature implies hostility. A love relationship inevitably deteriorates, and some of Banville's most lucid characters, understanding this, try to avoid the relationship. Thus the painter Marthe Biran in "La Doctoresse" (Dames et Demoiselles) tells the composer Paul Ternisien that love is for Romeos who have to die at twenty years of age. These two artists consciously decide not to be lovers, for, according to Marthe, that would have made them enemies. In its purest form, love "having no aim but itself is in fact the brother of death, with which the great Greek symbolists associated it in one and the same conception" ("Le Baiser," Contes heroïques, p. 94). Love is only a divine hope and if it does not end triumphantly in the delights of death it will lead to ignoble disenchantment ("Madame Robert," Madame Robert, p. 6).

Banville usually chooses to regard the imperfections of his own century from the point of view of caricature, comedy, wit, or a certain flippancy of attitude. He shows, for example, in "Histoire d'un règne" (Contes féeriques) how a poet would solve society's problems. The poet Roderic Parseval, having shown kindness to a stranger, who turns out to be the enchanter Nizery, is offered the kingship in the following amusing proclamation: "Citizen Roderic Parseval, lyric poet by profession, irreproachable rhymer, respectful of the supporting consonant and learned in the art of metrics, is invited to accept the position of King" (p. 397). He takes a poor law student as his minister and a woman of the people as his wife. He then carries through the following reforms: wine is no longer taxed, workmen get a discount on food purchases, large businesses are taxed, and the fine arts are supported by the state. Sometimes Banville is amusing through absurd oversimplification. For example, when Albert Eglem, newly arrived in Paris, asks his nephew to explain Paris to him in ten minutes, the latter defines Naturalists as writers who do not compose verse between their novels, or if they do, they imitate the versification and prosody of the great Alfred de Musset. The Parnassians, he adds, with more than a grain of truth, are poets whose only common bond is that their publisher is Alphonse Lemerre ("Documentaire," Les Belles Poupées).

Like Flaubert and other contemporaries, Banville regards as particularly characteristic of the bourgeois mentality its traffic in idées reçues. He presents a striking satire of this trait in "Séance de Portrait" (Contes féeriques). In it the devil comes to sit for the painter Gavarni. Tired of his Romantic aspect and his Byronic and fatal mask, he wants a modern Parisian image. As Gavarni draws, he does not copy the model, but rather the model conforms to his conception, becoming the image of the dandy, the incarnation of Parisian life. When the devil inquires how he may repay Gavarni, the latter asks for the gift of never drawing, saying, or even thinking anything commonplace. That will never please the bourgeois, the devil replies, for Gavarni is asking for the most precious of all gifts.

Another aspect of modern life that Banville deplores is the growth of technology. Like banality, technology erodes the autonomy of the individual and is the enemy of the creative spirit. In several of his stories he tries to imagine where a continuation of material progress may eventually lead, sometimes anticipating very nearly twentieth-century experiences. The most imaginative of these stories are "Mademoiselle Agathe" and "Voleur du feu," both from Contes féeriques. "Mademoiselle Agathe" presents the poet René de Siffroi as a "young Parisian from Paris and many other places, long-haired, witty, able to speak all the French languages and to understand not only current and modern matters but also those that do not yet exist" (p. 455). The demon Anizin takes him on a voyage to show him manifestations of progress. What he sees is that the whole universe is like a gigantic department store. Clerks are organized like an army. At the "live" toy counter fathers speaking in chorus as in a comedy of Aristophanes purchase wives for their sons. At another counter war ministers are shopping for armies, and so forth. But the poet prefers a place still untouched by progress.

"Voleur du feu" looks one hundred and fifty years into the future to the year 2030. In a sense anticipating the likes of George Orwell, it foresees interstellar and interplanetary travel, and governments dispensing light, water, heat, and even air for breathing. People have by this time become so accustomed to the loss of their individuality that, by a curious twist of Banvillean irony, one of the main concerns of 2030 is that individualism is threatening to replace "collective common sense." It is even rumored that someone, a new Prometheus, claims to have discovered an individual source of light and heat, a discovery certain to create a sensation. At this point the speaker proceeds to describe what we all recognize to be a candle, adding that these days no one can say how far progress will go.

In "Prudence" (Les Belles Poupées) we encounter the rather old idea that life is like a play, but with Banville's own variations. The main character, Joseph Hanne, makes the observation that life has a way of imitating art, specifically a play. The lyrical ecstasies of Act I inevitably lead to the ridiculous marriages, poisonings, or other catastrophes of the last act. Considering the interesting hypothesis that life could remain happy if it were not allowed to develop beyond Act I, Hanne sets out deliberately to direct his own life in such a way as to break the thread between the first act and the last one. He decides to spend a gold coin on something superfluous. Having bought some roses, a useless purchase in the sense that he knows no woman to whom he might offer them, he nonetheless conjures up an image of such a woman. Almost immediately and without any sense of surprise he meets her and gives her the roses. Now his main concern is not to see her again. But the next day at a ball in the British embassy, his cousin points out to him among the guests her childhood friend Henriette Fano, now widowed and recently arrived in Paris. Wonder of wonders, it is the lady of the roses! Joseph leaves immediately, dismisses his servants, and under an assumed name goes to settle in Meudon, all this to escape the continuation of Act I. In a year or so he learns that Henriette has been killed in an accident. Now he is sorry he did not act in just the opposite manner. Such is the result of all human prudence, he reflects, and "one cannot do anything over, not even what has not happened, and true wisdom consists in not seeing past one's nose."

The Artist

The most important characters in Banville's stories are artists, especially poets. More frequently than any other persons they appear as observers, narrators, or protagonists, and they constitute a valuable source of information about the nature of poetry or art in a wider sense and the place of the artist in the world. The poet Etienne Saignol in "Intermède" (Contes féeriques) makes us think of Banville's art. Gifted "with an extraordinary genius for comedy and an ability in the art of making French rhymes produce somersaults and tours de force which can bring joy to jaded minds, he willingly yields to a certain taste for farce which he has drawn from the old storytellers, and in the work of this charmer with words and phrases, admirer of Aristophanes, there is a bit of the caricaturist" (p. 114). Perhaps this charcterization of Saignol's talent also explains further why Banville was attracted to the old French _conte_. As we have seen over and over, there is also "a bit of the caricaturist" in Banville and much of the verbal acrobat with a taste for comic effects.

What is striking here is that this approach "can bring joy to jaded minds." Was the comic perspective a way of reaching a wider public? It is clear that reaching a wider public was not synonymous for Banville with being a popular writer. His conception of art as noble and lofty precludes any idea of easy success through compromise. The poet Claude Justel in "Le Rénégat" (_Contes féeriques_), inspired and instructed by the fairy Euryale, understands the superiority of "the magic power of the evocative harmony and invincible glory of the word" over that mediocrity that consists in "piling up platitudes of virtue and patriotism, taking pleasure in writing cacophonous and gray verses, in coupling silly and colorless rhymes, in making simple words rhyme with their compounds and short syllables with long syllables . . ." (p. 205). It is more likely that in speaking of jaded minds Banville was thinking of the mentality that accepts the commonplace at every turn. His desire to awaken such spirits was closely linked to what he regarded as the aim of poetry, perhaps nowhere better stated than by Saignol on the occasion of a poetry contest in the French Academy: "Poetry can have no other aim than itself, and if it can improve man it is by awakening in him the noble instinct of the beautiful, and not at all by any kind of demonstration . . ." (p. 119).

This high aim makes enormous demands of the artist and requires total concentration. Even love must take second place to art, for, as the painter Jacques Bianne explains in "Paysagiste" (_Madame Robert_), "one can satisfy only one master." The minimum that can be expected of a poet is summed up in a notable passage in "Innocence" (_Les Belles Poupées_):

> To grasp quickly an aspect of nature or life or the soul, to find the decisive words which must ex-

> press it and to plant these words in their place, in full light; to imagine a new, ingenious, and unexpected relationship between the two words of similar sound, which come to bill and coo at the end of the verse like doves; to subordinate to their essential sounds all the others in a varied and living symphony; to create a harmony at once more precise and less crude than that of music; to master all known rhythms, and if necessary, to create others; to make of the Word a painter, a sculptor, a delicate carver of arabesques; finally to imprison the infinite and to express the inexpressible; such are the minimum problems that the rhymer must solve, and to be sure, it is impossible to be lazy in order to devote oneself to that type of idleness. (pp. 157-58)

If this is an unattainable ideal, it is at least an ambition that the true artist places above all others. The British manufacturer, Archibald Pallock, who is really Satan, on a visit to Paris, where he has come "to obtain a distinguished and delicate soul," tempts the poet Gabriel Ram by offering him wealth and girls. But he is completely dumbfounded and defeated by the poet's reply that his ambition is much greater: "I should like, after having striven, worked, and learned my art, to succeed some day in writing ten consecutive good verses" ("Archibald," Les Belles Poupées, p. 269).

Like a number of other writers, Banville sees in the swan a suitable symbol of the poet. "Le Cygne" (Contes féeriques) begins with the story of the poet Daniel Berrus, fatally wounded in a duel with the bourgeois Edmond Loriol over a silly girl. Later, as a parallel to this incident, a swan, also fatally wounded by the same man, sings its song of death in words perfectly intelligible to the narrator and expressing the plight of the poet, formerly respected and now disdained: "Swans used to be gods and poets; they used to live among heroes and bearers of the lyre; but now, slaves on a ridiculous lake, we see, as they pass by, bourgeois on holidays, architects, merchants of wit who have no wit . . ." (p. 225). The bourgeois closes the story by explaining to the girl that swans are not "chic" and that they have the fault of recalling Virgil and poetry, which fortunately has been abolished.

The artist must resign himself to the prospect of being misunderstood and an outsider everywhere as long as he refuses to compromise his ideals. "You have to resign yourself to being an exile everywhere, a leper, a man strayed into the midst of a conspiracy of which he is not a part," says the painter Faugeron, in "Manette" (Les Belles Poupées, p. 184). This is true of all those rare beings for whom beauty is the highest good. However, since they cannot find it on earth in its purity and magnificent simplicity, the earth must remain for them a place of exile "where they suffer all the tortures of an eternal separation" ("Le Notaire," Contes héroïques, p. 173).

Marcelle Rabe

Published in the year of his death, Marcelle Rabe, Banville's only novel, resumes much of his philosophy of life relating to the corruption of the flesh and perhaps of the mind as well, but also to the beauty of effort and the greatness of sacrifice and willing renunciation. Madame Robert (1887) had prepared the way for the novel by treating the theme of the prostitute, corrupt in body but elevated by sacrifices made for the happiness of a man she really loves, an attitude illustrated especially in the title story "Madame Robert." It is explained in these terms: "That there is nothing else in life but duties is a truth so simple that it is not even worth enunciating; but it is also necessary to know how to choose, to accept lovingly the most stringent and difficult duty. To be a victim, to wish for martyrdom, is nothing but a joy for the person who has received the soul of an apostle; but to endure patiently the commonplaces, the follies, and the platitudes of daily life requires another kind of resignation" (pp. 70-71).

While the artist especially suffers as an exile amid the platitudes of daily life, the real martyrs in "Madame Robert" and in Marcelle Rabe are those whose suffering and sacrifices come from love. Marcelle Rabe and Suzanne Brunel, childhood friends from Dijon, where they were in the convent together, eventually go to Paris, where they make their living as prostitutes. Marcelle makes the acquaintance of the physician Daniel Mathis and they fall in love. She gives herself physically to Daniel but without offering any indication that she loves him. In order to keep her love pure and selfless she feels that she and Daniel should not continue to see each other, for she is eager not to corrupt him nor to place any obstacles in the way of his promising career. To try to make Daniel forget Marcelle, Suzanne arranges a meeting between him and Claudine Vandrenne, whom Daniel had met earlier and who is now the wife of a prosperous banker. This renewal of acquaintance signals the beginning of a series of sexual encounters and even orgies between the two. Near the end of the novel Marcelle sees Daniel one last time, admonishing him to seek the good and the true, and to cure mankind but without ostentation. "We have drunk and eaten the most vile filth, pretending it was ambrosia," she says, referring to their lives (p. 288), and then in a formula recalling Christ's miraculous healings, she addresses these parting words to him: "Now awaken and walk!"

Daniel, obsessed and blinded by desire, can be regarded as the incarnation of that human weakness which can make even the most powerful the slaves of the flesh. Claudine is more than a match for him in carnal appetite, but without any capability of lucid introspection. She is described as a "thirsty she-wolf with a fury for pleasure, subtle, cruel, impatient, greedy, the fashioner and creator of formidable joys" (pp. 168-69). The violence of her passion is such that Banville compares her to a soldier pillaging a captured town, and Daniel is like a woman being raped. In addition, she is a hypocrite. She does everything possible to create the image of chaste respectability. After their sexual episodes she dresses, not a hair out of place, and goes about her business as if nothing had happened. In her public role, at concerts, plays, and charities, she appears proper, smiling, innocent, and popular, with a compelling need to have people think her relationship with Daniel to be purely platonic. In a sense she is a split personality, and as Banville so quaintly puts it, "She was not really a liar, but in a naive way she was a stranger to reality" (p. 178). At her receptions Daniel comes to regard her as a she-devil dressed like a saint, but by a strange paradox during their sexual orgies he sees in her the innocence of childhood.

Marcelle, on the other hand, plays no role, but strives to be authentic. Her love for Daniel transforms her life. In order to sustain her purity she realizes that she and Daniel must remain separated and that she cannot accept his kisses: ". . . the purest kisses would awaken in his flesh and in mine the memory of the most vile kisses. I have burned, rejuvenated, and purified my soul in the flames of love; as for my body, irremediably soiled, it is necessary that it remain as if it were dead" (p. 216). In spite of her former life, her soul thirsts for purity. Her greatest wish is to see Daniel worthy of his destiny, and for this she gives up her former way of life and the easy pleasure of seeing him. Yet she seems somewhat like a Christian without grace. Nothing can remove the stains of her past. She must always keep in her heart "the heap of dung that infects and poisons it" (p. 65). For her, there is no easy path and no easy solution, but her resolute march toward the light and her lucid grasp of her condition, coupled with her example of uncomplaining renunciation in her earthly exile make her one of Banville's most admirable and lofty heroines.

Some Questions of Style

What of the qualities of Banville's prose? Let us first listen to the comments of two men who have each written a book on Banville. John Charpentier devotes several pages of glowing praise to the subject, calling Banville a "magnificent prose writer, incomparably gifted to narrate in a cheerful manner." He refers to his elegance of tone, his sublime harmony, his light and airy sentences, and the divine ease of his style. The moderation, naturalness, and purity of his prose is a "continuous enchantment," and even in its variety of moods, by turns mischievous and inspired, discreet and hyperbolic, clowning and enthusiastic, it remains light and unencumbered by verbiage, in spite of its richness of sounds and images (4).

In contrast to this tribute, Max Fuchs finds that Banville's prose tales add nothing to his glory, for "scarcely has the most indulgent and most kindly disposed reader read a few pages of it, when he is unpleasantly surprised by the negligence and slovenliness of the style, by the monotony of these meaningless and sometimes disagreeable fantasies" (5). Contrary to the disciplined language of his other works, his prose, according to Fuchs, is marred by the abuse of neologisms and familiar if not trivial expressions (6).

That two such apparently conflicting judgments exist would be more surprising if Banville's fiction were more widely known. It is often the case that the more a work is studied the more likely it is that a generally accepted body of critical opinion tends to emerge, accommodating some aspects of extreme views and rounding the sharp edges of divergent judgments. The fact is, however, that Banville's prose fiction has not been much studied and is not well known. There is as yet nothing that can be regarded as a body of critical opinion about it. Still the two judgments just cited are not totally irreconcilable. They are both based, and correctly so, on the recognition that Banville has adopted a familiar, conversational, and at times colloquial manner. This explains his use of neologisms and other expressions that might be offensive in a more elevated, solemn style, but these, I think, are in most instances quite in keeping with the tone he has chosen and especially with his penchant for verbal acrobatics. His writing, whether in prose or in verse, is rarely forced, ponderous, or clumsy. Ease and lightness are among its notable characteristics, but it is wrong to confuse them with "negligence and slovenliness." On the other hand, Charpentier's adjective "sublime" appears to be unsuitable precisely because of the generally familiar tone. If it is true, as Fuchs points out, that readers may find a certain monotony, perhaps this comes largely from the sheer number of tales, almost all of them of the same length, eight to ten pages, giving in the long run a certain impression of repetitiousness.

On the whole, his narrative technique is rather uniform. He usually begins with a conversation enunciating some hypothesis or idea, and then one of the speakers relates a story to illustrate it. To lend credibility to his tales, Banville sees to it that the narrator is a character who has actually experienced what is being related or has observed it. Banville takes the reader into his confidence and often gives an air of reality to the tale by making it seem that the starting point or other aspect of an event is common knowledge. For this purpose he finds the expression *comme on le sait* ("as everyone knows") particularly useful. Referring to the actress Rachel Sims, for example, he remarks, ". . . as everyone knows, the Marquis Gérard de Champlite fell in love with her, married her . . ." ("Arlequinade," *Contes pour les femmes*).

As he does for some of his plays and collections of

poetry, Banville supplies some kind of prologue or epilogue or both for almost every volume of his short stories, indicating the general nature of the book or commenting on an aspect of it. Thus the *dizain* opening *Contes pour les femmes* states that the subject of all its stories is "always you, ladies, dear readers," while the closing ballade declares, "I have narrated only for the ladies." The epilogue of *Contes bourgeois* comments that the subject of its stories is man, whose folly never dies. But the most interesting and imaginative of these epilogues occur as stories in their own right, forming part of a collection but constituting a fitting conclusion to it. Two striking examples can be cited. The first one is "Rue de l'Eperon," which closes *Contes féeriques*. In it fairies invade Banville's study (it will be remembered that Banville lived for a time on the rue de l'Eperon), telling him he must stop writing fairy tales because there is an ordinance against the supernatural and thus he is putting them into a difficult position. Besides, people are not comfortable if they see beneath appearances or if they think others can see beneath their exterior. "La Couveuse," the second example, is a commentary on the unheroic modern era. Pierrette Jauquin states that she can no longer find material to make people of important stature ("The clay on which I walk seems to be of bad quality"), and so *Contes héroïques* has to come to a close.

As for Banville's style generally in his short stories, the characteristics that many readers may find most striking, along with its ease and lightness, are its conciseness and economy. He has the ability to suggest a physical portrait by means of a carefully chosen detail or comparison. Consider, for example, this impression of Madame Schone in "Le Rat qui s'est retiré du monde" (*Fables choisies mises en prose* in *Dames et Demoiselles*): Her "little turned-up nose seemed to be trying to fly away like a bird" (p. 343). Similarly a few brush strokes can suggest a character, as we see in "La Fin de la fin" (*Contes pour les femmes*), where the shrewd maid Virginie is presented in this manner: "She was Parisian, deeply corrupted, having in her heart the seven capital sins and others as well, a skillful milliner, a grinder, a talented hairdresser, learned like a book, having perfect notions of good and evil, in order always to do evil, and on special occasions if necessary knowing how to cook in order to make people eat who ordinarily never eat" (p. 94). Such conciseness gives his narrative a rapidity sometimes recalling that of Voltaire's prose. In "Innocence" (Les Belles Poupées) the "innocent" Hughes Russignol has just entered an inn. The innkeeper's daughter Margot, at first sight of him, thinks to herself that this is the man for her. The narrator continues as follows: "Hughes was so innocent that he understood the glances of women as thoroughly as the song of birds. After having made a sign to Margot which meant 'Yes,' he entered the cabaret, asked the old drinker for the hand of his daughter, and after having shown his four hundred thousand francs, obtained it" (p. 163). The danger of this method may well be that, carried to extremes, it gives the impression of presenting a summary of a story rather than the story itself (7).

Banville's conciseness sometimes manifests itself in single-sentence portraits combining physical and moral attributes. These one-sentence formulae are not limited to portraits. Maxim-like pronouncements, proverbs, pastiches, and paradoxical statements are liberally sprinkled throughout his prose. A proverb, "Là où la chèvre est attachée, il faut qu'elle broute" (the goat has to graze where she is tied up), sums up the poet's acceptance of his lot in life ("Rue de l'Éperon," Contes féeriques, p. 473). His enigmatic comment on the rich widow, Henriette Septeuil, is that she "had all the virtues except one, which was absolutely lacking--virtue" ("Les Bourguignons," Contes héroïques, p. 111). It is a seeming paradox that, when the prostitute Jacqueline Chalvet, through the generosity of a virtuous man, is finally able to leave her profession behind, she leads a life of real pleasure: ". . . after having emptied the cup of ignoble misery, she thinks she has the right to savor a refined pleasure and she indulges in the unheard of luxury of living a chaste life" ("Ressuscités," Contes héroïques, p. 316). Occasionally the paradox is stated at the end of a narrative which has just illustrated it, as in "Un Début littéraire" (Contes féeriques). This is the story of the poet Eugène de Ledignan, who is remarkable because, taking no thought for the next day, he gives away his money to the needy, but finds there is always a coin caught in the mesh of his purse. He is simply unable to get rid of all his money "so difficult is it not to be rich."

Banville's style is never dull. His characters, though they may lack psychological depth, are alive. His narrative techniques are sound. But in spite of the rewards that readers can surely find in Banville's prose, they are likely to come away with the feeling that he is not primarily a storyteller. Paradoxically, the man so often accused of lacking ideas appears in his prose fiction to be more interested in the ideas illustrated by the stories than in the stories themselves. Readers may also be disconcerted by a sense of disorientation in Banville's world, which makes no distinction between an autonomous realm of fiction with its own realities and the world in which we live.

Chapter Eight

A Treatise on Poetry

A Theory of Poetry

In 1872 Banville published a curious book entitled *Petit Traité de poésie française*, the contents of which had already appeared in serialized form in the *Echo de la Sorbonne*. According to Max Fuchs, it was written as a textbook for schools, but Banville gives no indication that such was his intent (1). On the other hand, it has sometimes been regarded as a kind of Parnassian manifesto. Yet Banville does not claim to be a spokesman for any particular group or movement, and it would be difficult to support the view that his treatise fills a role comparable to that of such manifestos as Du Bellay's *Défense et Illustration de la langue française* or Hugo's *Préface de Cromwell*.

I have called it a curious book because in a sense it is like two separate books, each with a different purpose. The first part and the last chapter are of a theoretical and speculative nature, relating to the essence of poetry, its purpose, and the creative process. The middle is largely technical and could be regarded as a manual of versification. Much of this part is rather mechanical and reproduces what can be found in most manuals of versification. In this section Banville has borrowed liberally, for example, from Wilhelm Tenint's *Prosodie française*, Napoléon Bandais's *Dictionnaire des rimes*, Richelet's *Abrégé des règles de la versification française*, and Asselineau's *Histoire du sonnet*. Nonetheless, the sections on poems of fixed form seem to me to be particularly strong, reflecting Banville's interest in old rhythms and his expert knowledge of them.

Even this technical section is neither dull nor abstruse. Aided by his own lucid insight, Banville presents his material with clarity, and spiced with wit, images, and judicious use of examples. His obvious expertise is combined with a lightness of tone, which makes even polemical parts and seemingly paradoxical declarations pleasant to read. At times he deals with certain questions of versification in an unusually terse manner. For example, under the heading "Licences poétiques" there is only one sentence: "Il n'y en a pas" (There are none), and under the heading "De l'inversion" he puts "Il n'en faut jamais" (There must never be any). Although his unpretentiousness gives his technical explanations an air of nontechnical simplicity, this should not be mistaken for lack of knowledge, for his understanding of technique and especially of old verse forms is such that his treatise is still a useful reference work for questions of versification.

Like Sainte-Beuve, Banville regards the seventeenth and eighteenth centuries as nonpoetic, although he exempts such writers as Corneille, Molière, Racine, La Fontaine, and André Chénier from that judgment. In general, he says, French poetry between the sixteenth and the nineteenth centuries ought not to be read, "for it is already hard enough to write verse and it is always useless to read works that can only teach the way not to write verse" (2). The rhymes of the late eighteenth century are so monotonous that they would put quicksilver to sleep (p. 7). The target for most of his wit and satire is Boileau. Not only does Banville find many of the prescriptions in his "Art poétique" absurd and foolish, but he criticizes the quality of Boileau's verse, that "bad French of which he held the secret as soon as he spoke in verse" (p. 94).

It has been noted that in some ways Banville's _Petit Traité_ invites comparison with Boileau's "Art poétique" (3). Such an association, although Banville would have seen in it the greatest of ironies, is not without some validity. For one thing, there are some parallels in the general plan of the two works. Both begin with general principles, reserve the middle for the discussion of specific genres or forms, and end with practical recommendations and various other pieces of advice relating even to moral questions. Both in a sense can be regarded as handbooks useful to the apprentice wishing to learn the secrets of the master craftsmen. To a certain extent it can be contended that both summarize the practices of the good writers of their age. But here we must be wary. Banville thinks the practices of Corneille, Racine, and La Fontaine sometimes diverge sharply from some of those recommended by Boileau. Similarly, to note a number of similarities between the practices of some of the Parnassian poets and what Banville appears to recommend is not enough to justify the belief that he is their spokesman.

Whatever the parallels between Boileau and Banville may be, there is an essential difference--one of enormous importance. It is a basic difference in their conception of poetry. Banville's views on the nature of poetry are to be found in the less technical sections of his treatise, probably the most important but also the most misunderstood part of his Petit Traité. Indeed, I believe that a careful reading of it reveals a conception of poetry in some important ways rather different from that which is usually attributed to the Parnassians, and foreshadowing some ideas of the late nineteenth and early twentieth centuries.

In the preface to his Anthologie de la poésie française André Gide cites Banville's definition of poetry, which he finds "quite remarkable" and "perfect": ". . . that magic which consists in awakening sensations through the aid of a combination of sounds . . . that sorcery thanks to which ideas are necessarily communicated to us in a way that is certain by words that nevertheless do not express them . . ." (4). Although this definition does not come from the Petit Traité, it is the summary and concise formulation of ideas developed in more detail in the treatise. Gide might well have quoted the following passage from the treatise: "Poetry has as its aim to transmit impressions to the reader and to awaken images in his mind--but not by describing these impressions and these images. It is through an order of means far more complex and mysterious" (p. 269). These declarations could just as easily have come from Baudelaire or later Symbolists because they reveal a conception of poetry very close to theirs. Poetry for Banville is not just rhymed prose. He sees an essential characteristic of poetry in its communication through suggestion by means of "a combination of sounds," or as some might say, through sound patterns. Like Baudelaire, he recognizes the magic and the mystery in this type of communication. Like Verlaine, he gives priority to music or, as he prefers to call it, song.

Poetry for Banville is "the only complete and necessary art, and which contains all the others" (p. 11). It includes aspects of music, sculpture, painting, and eloquence; and it must charm the ear, enchant the mind, represent sounds, imitate colors, render objects visible, and arouse emotions (p. 11). It is essentially religious, for it addresses itself to what is most noble in us, our soul. In spite of his recognition of the inclusiveness of poetry, Banville constantly returns to the idea that it is song, declaring that "there is no poetry outside of song." Its purpose, he says, is to communicate "a music whose expression has been lost but which we hear in us, and which alone is Song" (p. 7). It is as necessary for us as the bread we eat and the air we breathe, for it is the expression of what is divine and supernatural in us and, if man could not sing, he would die (p. 7).

Such a conception of poetry leads Banville to certain corollaries. He shares with Ronsard the view that the poet must himself possess a certain moral elevation. He must have "the heart of a hero" filled with "an immense charity and an immense love" (p. 266). There is no room for selfishness; it will destroy not only the poet but also his poetry. The question of morality is of course connected with the concept of poetry as the expression of what is divine in man. Banville advances the axiom that atheism or the denial of our divine essence brings with it the suppression of all lyricism. It is the dominance of an atheistic presence that explains for him the inferiority of eighteenth-century poetry, which he calls "a dead thing."

Probably a more important corollary, and certainly a more modern one, is the concept of "pure poetry," which can perhaps be regarded as a logical extension of the idea of art for art's sake. Although Banville does not use the term "pure poetry," he identifies it in his own way. He does this first of all by recognizing a distinction in kind rather than merely in degree between prose and poetry. Poetry has its own distinct essence. The man who thinks in abstract terms will never succeed in translating his thought through a form. A real poet thinks in verse, whereas a mere versifier thinks in prose before translating into verse what he has thought in prose. The result is no better than a school translation exercise (p. 58). This being so, the test of pure poetry would be the absence of all prosaic or nonpoetic elements. In a sense, Banville seems to be saying that all lyric poetry is pure or it is not really poetry. Poetry should never try to do what another art or form of communication can do without it. Banville regards this question from a historical perspective, recognizing the necessity, before the invention of printing, of disseminating certain kinds of information in verse. But in modern times it is not the function of poetry to do what technical language can do better. The domain of poetry must remain limited to those functions where "it is indispensable and where nothing can replace it" (p. 160). Its purpose is not to describe, to narrate, to teach, or to moralize, if prose or technical language can do these things better.

A Misunderstanding about Rhyme

Probably the core of Banville's view of poetry is to be found in what he has to say about rhyme. This part of his treatise is perhaps the best known but ironically the least understood. It is possible that Banville's exaggerated rich rhymes, play on words, and other verbal acrobatics in his poetry may influence the reader's interpretation of his theories. His statement that "rhyme is the only harmony of verses and it is the whole verse" (p. 52), and his contention that rhyme should always be rich are widely known. On the basis of such pronouncements he is easily dismissed as the Parnassian theorist of rich rhymes or as a sort of nineteenth-century Grand Rhétoriqueur. But it is necessary to examine these ideas in their context and to consider Banville's explanations of them.

Banville begins his discussion of rhyme by quoting "A la rime" from Poésies de Joseph Delorme by Sainte-Beuve, whom Banville calls "the greatest critic of our time" and one of the best poets (p. 50). The very first stanza contains the key to the whole poem. It is that rhyme is "the sole harmony of the verse," and that it is the source or point from which the sounds emanate. Without it the verse would be mute. Banville takes this idea as a starting point, adding that rhyme is the whole verse and that it is really only the word at the rhyme that is heard in a verse. It is the word that produces the effect sought by the poet, whereas the other words in the verse fulfill the more passive role of not clashing with the effect of the rhyme word, of harmonizing with it, and forming various resonances with each other but of the same general color (p. 53). This explanation illustrates the importance of not taking Banville's pronouncements too literally and out of context. What he is really saying is, not that the rhyme word is literally the whole verse nor literally the only word that is heard, but rather that the whole verse has the rhyme word as its foundation, is shaped by it, and must not run counter to its general tonality, sound, and color.

That Banville eventually recognized the possibility that his sometimes terse pronouncements might be misinterpreted is indicated by the fact that he provides further explanations of some of them in other writings. For example, he tries to dispel the idea that rhymes should always be rich. While it is true that his Petit Traité appears to advocate rich rhyme, he might have added "as rich as possible considering the effect to be produced." In his article on the painter Emile Deroy he states that Deroy understood color in the same way Banville understood rhyme, "that is to say, not uniformly dazzling and rich, (according to the idea which fools attribute to us) but varied, diverse, lovingly joined to the thought, transfigured everywhere according to the nature of the subject treated . . ." (5). But his best elaboration can be found in one of his Lettres chimériques addressed to the critic Taine and bearing the title "La Rime" (6). In it he recalls a previous meeting with Taine at which the latter had asked his opinion of a statement made by an important poet to the effect that all is well if the verses end in beautiful sonorous rhymes, and that what they contain otherwise is of little importance. Banville's letter is a response to this question. He begins by saying that the poet's statement was elliptical and then proceeds to explain what the poet meant.

The explanation he gives is in fact a clarification of what he says about rhyme in his Petit Traité. While he does not add new concepts, he often expresses himself through comparisons. For example, in recognizing the popular misconception that to rhyme well is simply to rhyme richly, he states that that would be like saying that to be well dressed, a lady must always wear a low-necked gown of blue velvet. In reality, to be well dressed she must choose her attire according to the occasion. It is the same for rhyme, which must conform to the subject or the tone and must be as diversified "as the innumerable waves of the sonorous sea." Rhyme that is uniformly rich and commonplace is comparable to a bourgeois woman loaded down with coarse jewelry (7).

Recognizing that his concept of rhyme as the basis of the verse appears to be in direct conflict with Boileau's idea of the function of rhyme, Banville is at some pains to explain the difference between these two approaches, which relate to their differing views of the nature of poetry. According to Banville, Boileau and rhyme waged a ceaseless war against each other; they were never reconciled, or rather, they never knew each other. Not only were Boileau's own rhymes bad, but they dictated to him terms that did not express the ideas intended by him. Boileau represents for Banville the type of writer who thinks in prose, translates his ideas into a verse form, and tacks on a rhyme at the end of the verse. Far from being an obedient slave, as Boileau would wish, rhyme, according to Banville, is the generator of the verse. However, by this Banville does not mean that the poet should begin simply by aligning any words that rhyme richly and then fill the rest of the verse with whatever ideas can still be expressed. He does not see a master-servant relationship between rhyme and thought or idea. It is not a question of sacrificing rhyme to reason or reason to rhyme. For the poet, the two go hand in hand; they are one, and "as long as the poet truly expresses his thought, he rhymes well; as soon as his thought becomes confused, his rhyme also becomes confused, weak, tiresome, and commonplace" (p. 65). Banville sees in Boileau's method a separation between form and thought to the detriment of both, whereas in his own conception, form and thought in poetry tend to be inseparable, form being always the "Form of a Thought" (p. 270).

The beginning of the poetic process for Banville, then, is finding rhymes, for it is rhyme "that invents, imagines, combines, harmonizes, compensates. . . ." (8). The poet at this point is a more or less passive instrument of the Muse. He must remain humble and receptive, making certain that he in no way impedes the activity of that mistress. In other words, the selection of rhymes is largely a matter of inspiration. The greatest talent a poet can possess, the one with which a true poet is born, is what Banville calls "l'imagination de la rime" (p. 52). This appears to mean the ability to find rhymes that can anchor and project a pattern of sounds that, in combination with other elements of the poem, can exercise that mysterious magic that will suggest a vision or idea to the reader. He calls the rhyme word "this sorcerous word, this fairy word, this magic word, that must, like a subtle magician, bring before our eyes everything the poet wanted" (p. 55). He stresses the necessity of suggesting rather than describing or expressing in a logical or technical order. The poet must do as the painter does, who suggests the idea of a hedge without drawing or painting the contour or shape of the individual leaves.

In fact, the first requisite of a good rhyme is its suggestiveness. It must be chosen in such a way as to convey what is characteristic of the object, idea, or vision to be communicated. Although this is largely a matter of the poet's innate "imagination de la rime," the poet should have at his command a wide range of words. He should familiarize himself with history, theologies, philosophy, esthetics, the fine arts, and the trades, not so much for the sake of knowledge itself, but in order to be able to call things by their exact name, the _mot juste_, so that the words, especially those at the rhyme, will not be colorless, vague, or commonplace. He should read dictionaries and encyclopedias and learn the exact meanings, literal and figurative, of as many words as possible for, although the selection of rhyme words may be largely a matter of inspiration, the poet can, through his own efforts, ensure that he has a repertory from which the choice can be made.

Not only should the rhyme be as rich as possible, suggestive, and diversified, but it should present the element of surprise. Anyone can look in the dictionary and find two words that rhyme, and even rhyme richly. But the real test of a poet's rhymes consists in the discovery of unexpected relationships between two words of similar sound. Many of the rhymes in the seventeenth century and most of them in the eighteenth, according to Banville, lack that element. They are dull, uninspired, and tiresome. It is bad enough to make a word rhyme with a synonym, as for example _malheur_ and _douleur_, but two words of opposite meaning such as _malheur_ and _bonheur_ are no better, since a word automatically evokes a synonym or an antonym: "When one thinks of a white object, one can be surprised by the idea of a scarlet object, but not by the idea of a black object" (p. 81). It is a matter of finding between the two words "a relationship that is living, sudden, precise, ingenious, decisive, sublime in strength, in spirit or in good sense, or in anger, or in caressing tenderness, or in pain or in joy" (9). In the hands of a master like Victor Hugo, even seemingly commonplace rhymes like amour and jour, so overworked through the centuries, can be linked in new contexts and new associations to produce that element of surprise.

The foregoing idea is based on what for Banville is a universal principle governing the art of verse: variety in unity. The repetition of sounds at the end of the verse is one important aspect of that unity, but in order to achieve variety as many elements as possible of the rhyming words, apart from the sound, must be different, so as not to put the reader to sleep. To summarize that principle as regards rhyme, Banville offers this formulation: ". . . you will make rhymes as far as possible between words very similar in sound and very different in sense" (p. 80). He then proceeds to give specific recommendations, advising, for example, against rhymes between two nouns, two verbs, two adjectives, two adverbs, and between a word and one of its compounds. Although such "easy" rhymes had already been recognized as inferior at the time of Du Bellay and Ronsard, the reasoning underlying this view seemed somewhat vague. Banville's formula, however, is astonishingly modern. While in our day we encounter statements to the effect that rhyme is identity of sound in tension with semantic disparity, or that sounds approach each other while meanings diverge, such declarations stripped of jargon converge with Banville's own affirmation about sound and sense (10). Banville in his own way recognizes a poem as a verbal structure in which sound takes precedence over syntax as an organizing principle.

The Making of a Poem

As we have seen, rhyme is the starting point in the making of a poem. Banville deliberately uses the verb faire ("to make"), which he traces back to its Greek origins. He asks the question, "By what absolute and supreme characteristic shall we recognize then what is or what is not poetry?" (p. 7). His reply is that a poem is "that which is made and which consequently is no longer to be made." It is "a composition whose expression is so absolute, so perfect, and so definitive that no change whatever can be made in it without making it less good and without diluting the sense" (p. 7). He concedes, however, that this is more an ideal than a realistic expectation. Nonetheless, he is unwilling to give the name poetry to any composition that does not contain at least some parts that have that definitive perfection of expression that allows not a single word to be changed without diminishing its quality.

Much of what Banville says about the requisites of good rhyme is for the benefit of apprentices or those who have not been born with the kind of poetic endowment that characterizes such poets as Ronsard, La Fontaine, Racine, or Hugo. The "born" poet will instinctively begin with rhymes having the qualities Banville has identified. For such a poet the visions or ideas that come to his mind will be accompanied spontaneously by words that evoke or suggest them. These he will put at the rhyme. These evocative terms are furnished neither by common sense, nor logic, nor erudition, nor memory, but only by virtue of a special gift which is innate (p. 56). Not only does the evocative word representing the poet's vision arise spontaneously, but it presents itself along with a word that rhymes with it.

In his treatise Banville does not state clearly just how much of the poetic process is intuitive and how much can be learned. He appears to think that the clarity of the initial vision and the rhyme that evokes it cannot be acquired through learning. However, he sees a role for apprenticeship even for the born poet. Mastering his art will quicken his perceptions, allow him to recognize his visions more promptly, and help him perceive simultaneously entire sound patterns in a stanza. He will hear at the same time not only the accompanying rhyme word but all the rhymes of a stanza and, after that, all the characteristic and salient words which will be evocative. He will then hear also those words that are correlative to complete the sense and the harmony of the first words and that will form "with them a whole that is energetic, gracious, living, and solid" (p. 66). Thus the rhyme is the center of the universe that is the poem, and radiates the poet's vision to the various parts of the poem through words which join with it to maintain its unity of harmony, color, and meaning.

When the poet has proceeded that far, what remains?

Here is Banville's answer: "The rest, what has not been revealed, found that way, the connections, what the poet has to add in order to plug the holes with the hands of an artist and artisan, is what is called _chevilles_" (p. 66). The word _chevilles_ suggests both that which joins and that which fills. For Banville there is no poem without _chevilles_, which may be as numerous in a good poem as in a bad one. These connectives, it will be noted, do not form part of what has been "revealed" and thus are entirely a product of the poet's workmanship. It is possible to learn to become inventive and ingenious in producing these links.

Banville now turns again to the question of poetic endowment and apprenticeship. Can a writer born without the special gift of poetry learn to produce tolerable verse? Banville's answer is affirmative. This is possible because of our innate tendency to imitate. It is primarily for such writers that he stipulates certain rules, the first of which is that there is no poetic license. The poet must observe faithfully every grammatical rule even more so than the prose writer because poetry represents the most highly organized and rhythmic structure of language. A second important rule, perhaps really a special instance of the first, is that inversion is forbidden. He observes that, historically, inversion was widespread in times when writers did not know how to rhyme properly, and understandably so, because it was also in those times that poetic vocabulary was restricted, forcing writers often to do violence to the word order as a means of finding a word to complete a rhyme. Nine-tenths of French words, he adds, were "in quarantine or exiled" in the name of nobility of style (p. 71). But Victor Hugo has liberated them, providing sufficient choice for the poet and making it unnecessary to resort to inversion. In fact, Banville adds, there now exists an inexhaustible treasury of rhymes.

The second main step for the "nonpoetic" apprentice, after he has recognized the necessity of not taking liberties with grammar and word order, is to select and study a worthy model. This must be a single poet rather than all, or a large number of, poets. How could an apprentice hope to learn the methods, so often divergent or even contradictory, of several masters at the same time? That would be as foolish as being the apprentice of twenty master carpenters at the same time

(p. 75). Thus it is necessary to choose a single poet, the one who seems most compatible, and from his works the one that the apprentice admires most. He must then study it tirelessly "as a Lutheran reads his Bible" until he sees how his poet works (p. 75). In this way he will learn "as a child learns how to walk." The rhythm of the verse and the associations of sound will be assimilated in his mind and he will think and write in verse almost automatically. The apprentice can train himself further by forcing himself to find for each idea, sensation, object, aspect of nature, effect, or any combination of these, a single word that will characterize it, sum it up, or suggest it. This exercise will be completed by finding a word to rhyme with it.

An Evaluation

What Banville has to say about the apprenticeship of the would-be poet does not seem very convincing, and in any case it is debatable. Nourishing the mind by reading works of great poets and assimilating them is an idea that had been expressed by the poets of the Pléiade. But will this really enable the apprentice to think automatically in verse? And what of the choice of a single poet and even a single work to the exclusion of all others as models? Is the apprentice of poetry really comparable at this point with the carpenter? In Banville's defense, however, it can be pointed out that he does not claim that this process will result in originality or great poetry, only that "tolerable" poetry can come from imitation.

As a lexicon and handbook for technical aspects of versification, Banville's Petit Traité is still a useful reference. But its real value and interest lie in the theoretical sections. These are also the most controversial. That some of his ideas have been misunderstood is clear. In part, the fault is Banville's own in that some of his categorical and elliptical declarations discourage further investigation. The formula stands out so boldly that its nuances and real significance remain obscured. Weaknesses of detail can undoubtedly be found in the treatise, but its basic principles are its real strength and even originality. As Banville explains, his theory of rich rhymes has wider implications. He recognizes the importance of the phenomenon of rhyme in French verse, especially in shorter verses lacking a cesura. But his views on rhyme are really quite subtle and, in his parallel between commonplace rhymes and cheap jewelry, not so different from those Verlaine expresses in his "Art poétique."

The fundamental concept of poetry that emerges from the treatise is surely that it is a verbal structure organized primarily according to sounds. Verlaine's "De la musique avant toute chose" seems no more a Symbolist idea than Banville's insistence that poetry is song. Far from being a mere mechanical device, rhyme is the generator of suggestive evocation. Instead of being an obstacle to expression, it is its origin. He anticipates Valéry's judgment about rhyme and ideas: "Chances are much greater that rhyme will engender a [literary] 'idea' than to find the rhyme by beginning with the idea. This is the basis of all poetry and particularly that of the years 60 to 80" (11). Even if some of the details of Banville's explanation of how a poem is made are open to question, the important principle he enunciates is that of beginning with the rhyme. Although he does not say so explicitly, this method forces the poet to organize the poem according to sound patterns. It makes music, not discursive language, his first concern.

Another aspect of Banville's originality is his understanding of the concept of pure poetry well before the celebrated debates involving such figures as the Abbé Bremond and Valéry. His vocabulary is not that of the twentieth century, but his understanding of the subject again anticipates Valéry. Like Valéry he sees clearly the limits of pure poetry. The best a poet can hope for is to obtain a number of poetic fragments, that is, verbal groups of pure poetry. These the poet must then link together, as we have seen, with what Banville calls _chevilles_. Prosaic elements can never be completely excluded, as Valéry also concedes: "In sum, what we call a poem is composed in practice of fragments of pure poetry set in discursive matter" (12).

Banville's treatise is not closely and lucidly argued as Valéry's prose is. Even in his treatise, he shows his fondness for verbal clowning. His tone is anything but academic. These facts, together with his reputation as a writer lacking ideas, may explain in part why his treatise has not been taken more seriously. It may be that he himself did not see, except perhaps intuitively, all the implications of what he had to say. Yet it is difficult not to see in his *Petit Traité* some of the most important principles accepted by the French Symbolists and some of their early twentieth-century successors.

Chapter Nine
Conclusion

A Poet's Poet

Théodore de Banville's death in 1891 did not make a great impression in Paris. Although the press devoted a few articles to him in praise of his integrity and of his character generally, none mentioned his writing and none spoke of him as an ardent and noble artist. Banville would have regarded this as a cruel irony. Many times he had proudly proclaimed himself to be a lyric poet, for him the highest calling in life, and now he was being recognized as a man rather than as a poet.

By most standards his life could be judged a success. His childhood had been unusually happy, he had enjoyed the friendship and affection of many of his contemporaries, his marriage had been a happy one, his work as a columnist had not been unrelated to his interest in theater and poetry, and he had been endowed with a sunny outlook on life. But his creative writing generally had not been widely recognized during his lifetime. Some of his plays had never been performed and others rarely. His prose fiction had scarcely been noticed, and to this day is little known. Although some of his lyric poetry fared better, it had no wide appeal. His artistic standards were uncompromising.

But the recognition denied him by many critics and the public generally came in warm laudatory terms from some of his colleagues, particularly from two of the most outstanding French poets of the second half of the nineteenth century: Mallarmé and Baudelaire. Both were personal friends of Banville; both respected him as a poet as well, admiring the lyric quality of his verse.

Mallarmé refers to him as "the divine Théodore de Banville, who is not a man, but the very voice of the lyre," a voice which intensifies in Mallarmé a love of life and of beauty and makes him proud to be a human being. He regards Banville as the incarnation of the ageless poet in the lineage of Orpheus and Apollo:

> It is because in our time this man represents the poet, the eternal and classical poet, faithful to the goddess and living amid the forgotten glory of heroes and gods. His word is an endless song of enthusiasm from which spring music and the cry of the soul drunk with all glory. The sinister winds that speak in the terror of the night, the picturesque abysses of nature--these he neither wants to hear nor must he see them: he walks like a king through the Edenic enchantment of the golden age, celebrating for all time the nobility of the rays and the redness of the roses, the swans and the doves, and the dazzling whiteness of the young lily, --the happy earth! This is how he must have been who first received the lyre from the gods and spoke the blinded ode ["l'ode éblouie"] before our ancestor Orpheus. Thus Apollo himself. (1)

Baudelaire's assessment is not so different from Mallarmé's. Baudelaire finds that one of the words occurring most often in Banville's poetry is "lyre" and that "Banville's talent is essentially, decidedly, and voluntarily lyrical." He proceeds to explain that the lyrical mood or vision tends toward hyperbole to express a heightened state of life, and regards things in their general and universal aspect. In many ways Banville is untouched by the particular manifestations of life in his century. He is situated in that lineage of poets who see the aim of art in "the enchantment of the spirit." According to Baudelaire, modern art has an essentially demonic tendency to which the melancholy and incurable despair of the nineteenth century are related. But Banville has not entered that domain:

> But Théodore de Banville refuses to incline toward these bloody swamps, these muddy abysses. Like the art of antiquity, he expresses only what is beautiful, joyous, noble, great, rhythmic. Therefore, in his works you will not hear the dissonances, the discordances of the music of the witches' sabbath, no more than the yelping of irony, that vengeance of the vanquished. In his verse everything has a festive and innocent air, even an air of ecstasy. His poetry is not only a regret, a nostalgia, it is even a very willing return toward the state of paradise. From this point of view we can consider

> him then as an original [poet] of the most courageous nature. Right in the middle of a satanic and Romantic atmosphere, in the middle of a concert of imprecations, he has the audacity to sing the goodness of the gods and to be a perfect classic. (2)

The judgments of these two great poets point to the real Banville, the singer of songs, the lover of beauty, whose poetic world is bathed in the innocent light of paradise. The real Banville, however, is not always easy to find. Superficially his poetry comes to us in many forms. His rondels are in the manner of Charles d'Orléans, his ballades imitate Villon, his *Occidentales* make us think of Hugo's *Orientales*, many poems in his *Améthystes* are built on rhythms of Ronsard, a considerable part of *Les Cariatides* is in the spirit of Musset, and some of the poems of *Le Sang de la Coupe* recall Baudelaire. The mixture of pagan and Christian elements, of the real world and of a fairy world, may be jarring for some readers, but it has its peculiar charms. These opposing elements are often not fused or reconciled; they simply coexist.

Although, as we have seen, Banville sometimes refers to the complexity of modern life, his attempts to convey that complexity usually result in an image of man and society that, in spite of references to vices, really fails to take into account the depth of human perversity, as Baudelaire does, for example. The sense of sin and guilt also appears foreign to Banville's idea of man. Equally lacking is the feeling of mystery and anguish. His most pervasive view is that of man as an exile from his true home, but not as a fallen creature. In a sense man has brought with him into his exile his joy, and he regards this exile as a sacrifice to be accepted willingly and even cheerfully. Although he may have been right in seeing the ironic vision as a modern one, I am not convinced that it agreed with his temperament. Much of that writing that I have usually termed "funambulist" appears to have been an attempt to accomplish what he said Heine had done. But at heart Banville is really not a satirist. He is interested more in the achievement of comic effects through art than he is in reforming society. Banville the satirist is not the Banville admired by Baudelaire and Mallarmé.

In a sense the real Banville can be found in almost

everything he wrote because it is almost all lyrical. But in much of his writing his lyricism appears in combination with elements less characteristic of him, such as buffoonery, satire, and pastiche. It is unfortunate that he is so often regarded as the poet of the Odes Funambulesques rather than the poet of Les Exilés. The latter is not only the collection Banville himself preferred but also one in which his lyricism is attended by the smallest number of extraneous and nonlyrical elements. It is here as well as in much of the other "non-funambulist" poetry, in much of his theater, and in some of his prose fiction, that he sings the beauty of life and the nobility of man's sacrifice. Those who require some sort of political or social message in a writer and those who look for an expression of the anguish and tragedy of existence will be disappointed in Banville. But it is difficult to think of any poet who more consistently exalts the noble calling of the artist and sings because of the beauty of the sounds and the joy of living.

Influences

Banville's influence must be termed modest at best. He founded no school, had no major disciple, and did not affect the evolution of poetry in any significant way, as Baudelaire or Hugo can be said to have affected it. His own masters included Ronsard, Hugo, Heine, and Gautier. Ronsard was for him the embodiment of the true meaning of poetry. He regarded Hugo as the greatest poet, a model to be emulated, the fount of poetic wisdom. Although his admiration came close to worship, he did on occasion find imperfections even in the master. Heine represented the spirit of modern life for him and ranked just below Hugo. Banville's respect for Gautier came from the latter's recognition of the importance of craftsmanship and his philosophy of art for art's sake.

Banville's impact on French literature was limited. It is true that through personal contact and warmth of personality he encouraged some of the young writers of his time. Albert Glatigny, for example, was one of his most fervent admirers and is said to have become a poet after reading Banville's Odes Funambulesques. Glatigny, together with Armand Silvestre, Laurent Tailhade, and Tristan Derème, none of them first-rate poets, could possibly be regarded as disciples of Banville. For Verlaine, Banville opened the world of Watteau and the <u>fêtes galantes</u>; and his Pierrot reappears in Verlaine and Laforgue. His idea of rehabilitating old popular songs was taken up by Vielé-Griffin, and Edmond Rostand's heroi-comic theater recalls some of Banville's plays. Furthermore, Banville anticipated some of the objectives of Jean Moréas and the École Romane in his attempt to link modern poetry with traditions going back to the Pléiade and Greek antiquity.

Within the group of poets known as Parnassians, Banville's role has perhaps been overrated. Although he was one of the older members, he was constantly overshadowed by Leconte de Lisle, who was as domineering as Banville was mild-mannered. He was not assertive and self-promoting and did not always receive the credit he deserved. It is unfortunately so often forgotten, for example, that the ideas in Gautier's famous "L'Art" come from a poem by Banville to which "L'Art" is merely a reply (3). As a poet he incorporated some of the ideas of the Parnassians. Though he wrote with ease, he was a strong believer in the importance of craftsmanship. He shared with many of his colleagues a dislike for his own age and an admiration for Greek antiquity. He lacked the erudition of Leconte de Lisle and Heredia and his talent was not in the realm of epic poetry. His wit and humor stood out in noticeable contrast to the gravity of some of the Parnassians. On the other hand, he was one of the most faithful adherents of the doctrine of art for art's sake.

Both in theory and in practice Banville in some ways goes beyond the Parnassians. As a master of rhythms and sounds he produced in his own work much verse that has a fluid and suggestive quality. While in some of his poems he expresses the ideal of sculptural beauty, his very concept of poetry is based on the idea of the primacy of music. His notion of rhyme, it seems to me, has been largely misunderstood, and his references to rich rhyme have been dismissed as a Parnassian idea of solidity of form. Yet he clearly states that the main function of the rhyme word is to suggest and that the rest of the verse must be constructed to achieve a harmonious pattern of sound. These are modern ideas. They are Symbolist ideas. While literary history has given little recognition to this fact, some of

Banville's younger contemporaries were aware of it. Charles Morice and Gustave Kahn, for example, acknowledged a debt to him (4), and it was Anatole France, referring to Banville, who declared, "The Symbolists tried to realize the dreams, the desires of our most singing poet" (5).

Whatever its faults, Banville's Petit Traité de poésie française in its fundamental ideas was ahead of its time and deserves to be taken more seriously as a document in the history of Symbolism. Although Banville's characters in fiction and in theater are not usually psychologically unforgettable, there is a certain nobility and moral greatness in many of them. The beauty of the poetry makes his theater worthy to rank high in the repertory of lyric theater in France. His prose fiction, though difficult to characterize, deserves to be better known. But above all, Banville is a poet, a virtuoso of words. Perhaps it is important that now and then in human history someone should come along to remind us that beauty is the poet's first concern, to illustrate the wealth of technical and formal resources available to the poet, and to demonstrate that "song is nothing but the nostalgia for what exists beyond our intelligence and our senses . . ." (6).

Notes and References

Chapter One

1. Anatole France, "Théodore de Banville," La Vie littéraire, 4e série, in Oeuvres complètes illustrées (Paris: Calman-Lévy, 1925), 7:600-601.
2. Banville, "Portraits de famille," Mes Souvenirs (Paris, 1883), p. 7.
3. Banville, Oeuvres (Genève, 1972), 2:3. Unless otherwise stated all references to Banville's Oeuvres will be to this edition; hereafter cited as Oeuvres. Quotations from Oeuvres will normally be followed by volume and page numbers.
4. Banville, Mes Souvenirs, pp. 20-21.
5. Banville, "Préfaces," Critiques, choix et préface de Victor Barrucand (Paris, 1917), p. 463.
6. Charles-Augustin Sainte-Beuve, "Poésies complètes de Théodore de Banville," Causeries du lundi (Paris, n.d.), 14:82-85. The poem in question is entitled "A la Font-Georges" and is found in Les Stalactites.
7. For Banville's impression of this part of his life see his "Le Théâtre Comte," Mes Souvenirs, pp. 22-28.
8. Banville, Mes Souvenirs, p. 25.
9. Ibid.
10. Banville, "Les anciens Funambules au boulevard du Temple," Mes Souvenirs, p. 219.
11. Banville, Mes Souvenirs, p. 12.
12. Banville, "A la Muse," Oeuvres, 7:203. It may be noted that Banville frequently writes the words rythme and rime with an h.
13. Banville, "Le Théâtre Comte," Mes Souvenirs, p. 27.

Chapter Two

1. Oeuvres, 5:i.

2. Banville, "Henri Heine," Mes Souvenirs, pp. 443-44.

3. Victor Hugo, Oeuvres poétiques (Paris: Gallimard, 1964), 1:919.

4. See Théophile Gautier, "Les Progrès de la poésie française depuis 1830" in Histoire du romantisme (Paris: Charpentier, 1877), p. 301, and Charles Baudelaire, "Théodore de Banville," Oeuvres complètes (Paris, 1975), 2:162-69.

5. John Charpentier, Théodore de Banville, l'homme et son oeuvre (Paris, 1925), p. 247.

6. Max Fuchs, Théodore de Banville, 1823-1891 (Paris, 1912), p. 43.

Chapter Three

1. Oeuvres, 8:281-333.

2. Oeuvres, 2:5.

3. For Sainte-Beuve the four-syllable verse ending each stanza suggested the sound of the bell of Banville's native village and he admired the "indecision and even vagueness" of the ending of the poem, leaving the reader in a state of revery. See his "Poésies complètes de Théodore de Banville," 14:82, 85.

4. Charpentier, Banville, p. 155.

5. Oeuvres, 2:99-100.

6. Ibid., p. 101.

7. Fuchs, Banville, p. 159.

8. Oeuvres, 2:103.

9. Oeuvres, 1:1.

10. "Commentaire," Oeuvres, 1:296.

11. Quoted by Robert Sabatier, La Poésie du XIXe siècle (Paris, 1977), 2:30.

12. Banville, Mes Souvenirs, p. 302.

13. Banville, "Lamartine," Critiques, pp. 111-12.

14. Banville, Mes Souvenirs, pp. 439-45.

15. On this point see Baudelaire, "Théodore de Banville," Oeuvres, 2:167.

16. See also Fuchs's discussion of this poem, Banville, pp. 194-95.

17. Banville, "Innocence," Les Belles Poupées (Paris, 1888), p. 158.

18. Oeuvres, 6:169.

19. Oeuvres, 3:235.

Chapter Four

1. Banville, "Préface," Le Sang de la Coupe in Oeuvres, 6:4.

2. Ibid., pp. 3-6.

3. Ibid., p. 6.

4. In "Erinna," Les Exilés, Oeuvres, 7:103, Banville has this to say about feminine rhymes: "Et j'ai rimé cette ode en rimes féminines / Pour que l'expression en restât plus poignante" (And I have rhymed this ode in feminine rhymes in order that its expression might remain more poignant).

5. Oeuvres, 7:5; hereafter page references cited in the text.

6. According to Italo Siciliano, Dal Romanticismo al Simbolismo: Théodore de Banville, Poeta, Commediografo, Prosatore (Torino, 1927), p. 160, note 3, the marriage took place on February 18, 1865. To my knowledge this is the only study that gives that date.

7. Banville, La Lanterne magique. Camées parisiens. La Comédie française (Paris, 1883), p. 411.

8. Oeuvres, 7:215; hereafter page references cited in the text.

9. Oeuvres, 3:151; hereafter page references cited in the text.

Chapter Five

1. Oeuvres, 4:4-5; hereafter page references cited in the text.

2. Ibid., p. 4.

3. Cited by Banville in his Oeuvres, 7:304.

4. Ibid., p. 315.

5. Reported by Max Fuchs, Banville, p. 310.

6. Oeuvres, 5:300; hereafter page references cited in the text.

7. See Charpentier, Banville, pp. 116-17.

8. Banville, "Avant-Propos," Nous Tous (Paris, 1884).

9. See for example "Deux Tours" and "Thalie" in Sonnailles et Clochettes (Paris, 1890).

Chapter Six

1. Banville, "Avant-Propos," Comédies (Paris,

1879, p. I.

2. See Banville's "La Leçon de Balzac," _Critiques_, p. 454, and also his column in _Le National_ of August 19, 1872.

3. Banville, _Critiques_, p. 253.

4. Banville, "Avant-Propos," _Oeuvres_ (Genève, 1972), 9:ii.

5. Ibid.

6. Banville, _Mes Souvenirs_, pp. 216-17.

7. _Oeuvres_, 9:iii.

8. Banville, _Mes Souvenirs_, p. 441.

9. Ibid., p. 372.

10. On this point see Fuchs, _Banville_, pp. 400-401.

Chapter Seven

1. Banville, _La Lanterne magique. Camées parisiens. La comédie française_ (Paris, 1883), p. 185.

2. Banville, _Contes pour les femmes_ (Paris, 1881), pp. i-ii; hereafter page references cited in the text.

3. Charpentier, _Banville_, p. 236.

4. Ibid., pp. 217-20.

5. Fuchs, _Banville_, p. 444.

6. See notes in Fuchs p. 445, for examples.

7. See, for example, "Le Poète," _Contes pour les femmes_.

Chapter Eight

1. Fuchs, _Banville_, p. 422.

2. Banville, _Petit Traité de poésie française_ in _Oeuvres_ (Genève, 1972), 8:74; hereafter page references cited in text.

3. Edmondo Rivaroli, _La Poétique parnassienne d'après Théodore de Banville_ (Paris, 1915), p. 19.

4. André Gide, _Anthologie de la poésie française_ (Paris: Gallimard, 1949), p. 50. The definition comes from Banville's article on Ronsard, _Oeuvres_, 8:298.

5. Banville, _Mes Souvenirs_, p. 93. The same idea is expressed by the critic Secrétan in "Le Renard et les raisins," _Dames et Demoiselles_ (Paris, 1886), pp. 300-301.

6. Banville, "La Rime," Lettres chimériques (Paris, 1885), pp. 78-84.

7. Ibid., p. 82.

8. Ibid., p. 79.

9. Ibid., p. 83.

10. See for example Jean Cohen, Structure du langage poétique (Paris: Flammarion, 1966).

11. Paul Valéry, "Cahiers B 1910," Oeuvres (Paris, 1960), 2:582.

12. Valéry, "Poésie pure," ibid., 1:1957.

Chapter Nine

1. For these references to Mallarmé's opinions see his "Symphonie littéraire," Oeuvres complètes (Paris, 1945), pp. 264-65.

2. For these references to Baudelaire's opinions see his "Théodore de Banville," Oeuvres, 2:168-69.

3. It is with some surprise that I note that Edmondo Rivaroli in his La Poétique parnassienne, erroneously regards Banville's poem as the reply to Gautier's "L'Art."

4. According to Charpentier, Banville, p. 199.

5. France, "Théodore de Banville," Oeuvres, 7:529.

6. Banville, Critiques, p. 278.

Selected Bibliography

To date there is no edition of Banville's complete works. Translations into English and critical editions of single works are almost totally lacking. The following is a list of editions used or referred to in this study. Original dates of publication if other than those given here can be found in Chronology. Place of publication is Paris unless otherwise stated.

PRIMARY SOURCES

L'Ame de Paris. Nouveaux Souvenirs. Charpentier, 1890.

Les Belles Poupées. Charpentier, 1888.

Comédies. Charpentier, 1879.

Contes bourgeois. Charpentier, 1885.

Contes féeriques. Charpentier, 1882.

Contes héroïques. Charpentier, 1884.

Contes pour les femmes. Charpentier, 1881.

Critiques. Edited by Victor Barrucand. Charpentier, 1917. Contains a selection of articles by Banville.

Dames et Demoiselles. Charpentier, 1886.

Dans la Fournaise. Charpentier, 1892.

Esope. Charpentier et Fasquelle, 1893.

Gringoire. Calmann-Lévy, 1914.

La Lanterne magique. Camées parisiens. La Comédie française. Charpentier, 1883.

Lettres chimériques. Charpentier, 1885.

Madame Robert. Dreyfous, 1887.

Marcelle Rabe. Charpentier, 1891.

Mes Souvenirs. Charpentier, 1883.

Nous Tous. Charpentier, 1884.

Oeuvres. 9 vols. Geneva: Slatkine Reprints, 1972. These nine volumes reproduce the Lemerre editions of the 1890s of most of Banville's poetry and plays together with his Petit Traité de poésie française, articles on Ronsard and La Fontaine, and five articles on Banville by Barbey d'Aurevilly, Baudelaire, Gautier, Sainte-Beuve, and Tellier.

Paris vécu. Feuilles volantes. Charpentier, 1883.
Socrate et sa femme. Calmann-Lévy, 1885.
Sonnailles et Clochettes. Charpentier, 1890.
Les Stalactites. Edited by Eileen Souffrin. Didier, 1942.

SECONDARY SOURCES

BAUDELAIRE, CHARLES. "Théodore de Banville." In Oeuvres complètes, edited by Claude Pichois, 2:162-69. Gallimard, 1975. A penetrating analysis of the special qualities of Banville's poetry by one of his best friends.

CHARPENTIER, JOHN. Théodore de Banville, l'homme et son oeuvre. Perrin, 1925. A sensitive general study of Banville and his work. Sympathetic toward Banville and perhaps at times too uncritical. Sees Banville as a transition figure.

DENOMME, ROBERT T. The French Parnassian Poets. Carbondale and Edwardsville: Southern Illinois University Press; London and Amsterdam: Feffer and Simons, 1972. Situates Parnassian poetry in the positivist and realist current. Good studies of some individual poets of the time, including Banville.

ESTEVE, EDMOND. Le Parnasse. Centre de documentation universitaire, 1929. Contains useful information on earlier works of Banville.

FUCHS, MAX. Théodore de Banville, 1823-1891. Cornély, 1912. The most complete piece of research on Banville so far. A well-balanced study of all of his work.

GRANT, ELLIOTT M. "Théodore de Banville as a Poet of Revolt." Philological Quarterly 4 (October, 1925):373-80. Describes Banville's poetry as a protest against materialism.

GREIN, HEINRICH. Studien über den Reim bei Théodore de Banville. Ein Beitrag zur Geschichte der französischen Verstechnik. Kiel: Robert Cordes, 1903. Examines rhymes, specifically in Les Cariatides, the Odes Funambulesques, Les Exilés, and Idylles Prussiennes.

LAPORTE, A. Théodore de Banville: Etude bibliographique de ses éditions originales, précédée d'une notice littéraire sur ses oeuvres. Laporte, 1884. A useful reference but does not include Banville's later works.

LEMMONIER, LEON. "Edgar Poe et Théodore de Banville." Revue de littérature comparée 6, no. 4 (October-December, 1926):688-90. Tries to demonstrate that Banville borrowed the idea of rhyme as the generator of poetry from Poe.

MALLARME, STEPHANE. "Symphonie littéraire." In Oeuvres complètes, edited by Henri Mondor and G. Jean-Aubry, pp. 264-65. Gallimard, 1945. A lucid analysis of the effects of Banville's poetry by a poet who understood Banville.

MARTINO, PIERRE. "Théodore de Banville." In Parnasse et Symbolisme, pp. 24-28, and p. 30. Armand Colin, 1958. A short introduction to Banville, combining basic information with a succinct assessment of his work.

RIVAROLI, EDMONDO. La Poétique parnassienne d'après Théodore de Banville. Maloine, 1915. Useful study of Parnassian poetics but not a very penetrating analysis of Banville's Petit Traité de poésie française.

ROBERTS, MARGARET MARY. Théodore de Banville: The Poet and his Work. Ph.D. dissertation, University of Toronto, 1971. A close study of some of Banville's writings through an examination of a number of important themes. Tends to overestimate Banville's role as a social critic.

SABATIER, ROBERT. "Banville le funambule." In La Poésie du XIXe siècle, 2:27-38. Albin Michel, 1977. One of the best chapters on Banville, remarkable for the richness of insights compressed into so few pages. The study does not examine Banville's prose, however.

SAINTE-BEUVE, CHARLES-AUGUSTIN. "Poésies complètes de Théodore de Banville." In Causeries du Lundi. Garnier, n.d. 14:69-85. A penetrating study based on Banville's first four collections of poetry. Even so early in Banville's career, Sainte-Beuve discovers the suggestive qualities of Banville's poetry.

SCHAFFER, AARON. The Genres of Parnassian Poetry. A Study of the Parnassian Minors. Baltimore, Md.: Johns Hopkins Press; London: Humphrey Milford; Paris: Société d'édition "Les Belles Lettres," 1944. Useful section on Banville including a good summary of other critics' opinions of him.

SICILIANO, ITALO. Dal Romanticismo al Simbolismo:

Théodore de Banville--Poeta, Commediografo, Prosatore. Torino: Bocca editori, 1927. Another general study ranging over all of Banville's work. Contains some biographical information conflicting with that found elsewhere.

SOURIAU, MAURICE. *Histoire du Parnasse*. Spes, 1929. Still probably the best-known and most complete history of the Parnassians in France.

VINCENT, FRANCIS. "Théodore de Banville." In *Les Parnassiens. L'Esthétique de l'école. Les Oeuvres et les hommes*, pp. 118-33. Gabriel Beauchesne, 1933. Sees Banville as a poet belonging to the Parnassians more in body than in spirit.

Index